SUMMER STUDY

GRADE

K

New York

New York

An Imprint of Sterling Publishing
1166 Avenue of the Americas
New York, NY 10036

ISBN 978-1-4114-7862-6

Distributed in Canada by Sterling Publishing Co., Inc.
c/o Canadian Manda Group, 664 Annette Street
Toronto, Ontario, Canada M6S 2C8
Distributed in the United Kingdom by GMC Distribution Services
Castle Place, 166 High Street, Lewes, East Sussex, England BN7 1XU
Distributed in Australia by Capricorn Link (Australia) Pty. Ltd.
P.O. Box 704, Windsor, NSW 2756, Australia

For information about custom editions, special sales, and premium and corporate purchases, please contact Sterling Special Sales at 800-805-5489 or specialsales@sterlingpublishing.com.

Manufactured in Canada
Lot #:
2 4 6 8 10 9 7 5 3 1
03/16

www.flashkids.com

Dear Parent,

As a parent, you want your child to have time to relax and have fun during the summer, but you don't want your child's math and reading skills to get rusty. How do you make time for summer fun and also ensure that your child will be ready for the next school year?

This Summer Study workbook provides short, fun activities to help children keep their skills fresh all summer long. This book not only reviews what children learned during preschool, it also introduces what they'll be learning in kindergarten. Best of all, the games, puzzles, and stories help children retain their knowledge as well as build new skills. By the time your child finishes the book, he or she will be ready for a smooth transition into kindergarten.

As your child completes the activities in this book, shower him or her with encouragement and praise. You can feel good knowing that you are taking an active and important role in your child's education. Helping your child complete the activities in this book is providing an excellent example—that you value learning every day! Have a wonderful summer, and most of all, have fun learning together!

Match Up

Circle the picture in each row that matches the first picture.

Sunny Circles

Find the circles. Then draw a line from each to the middle.

Amazing Maze

Follow the pictures whose names start with **A** to solve the maze.

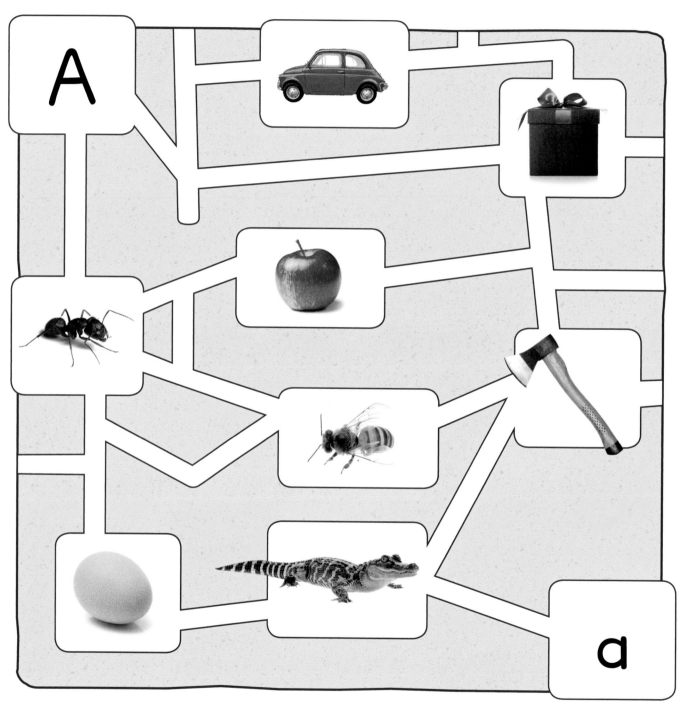

Trace and write.

A a

Lots of Lemonade

Count the cups of lemonade on each line. Write the numbers.

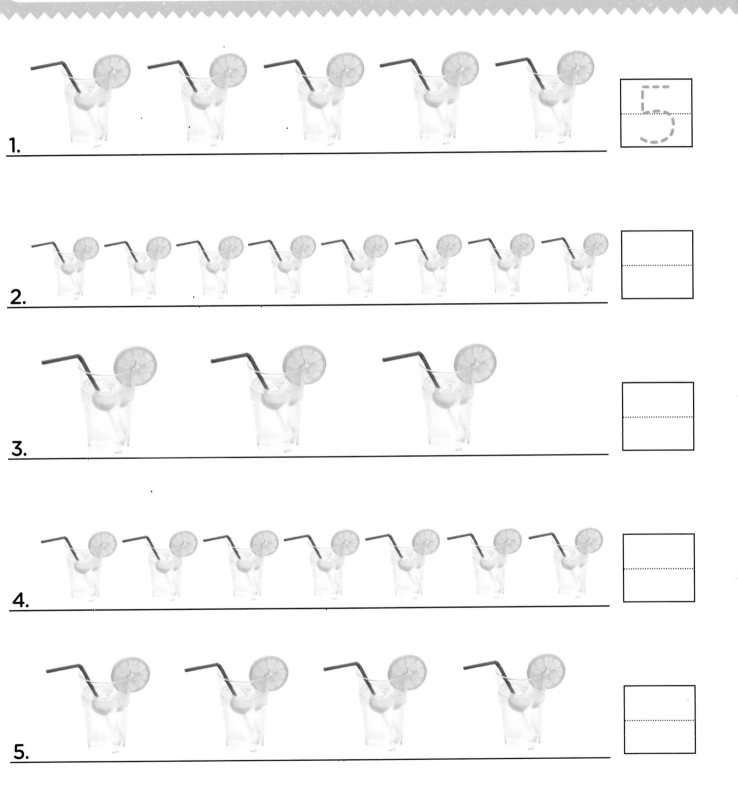

1.

2.

3.

4.

5.

Oranges! Oranges!

Count the oranges in each group.
Circle the group in each box that has more oranges.

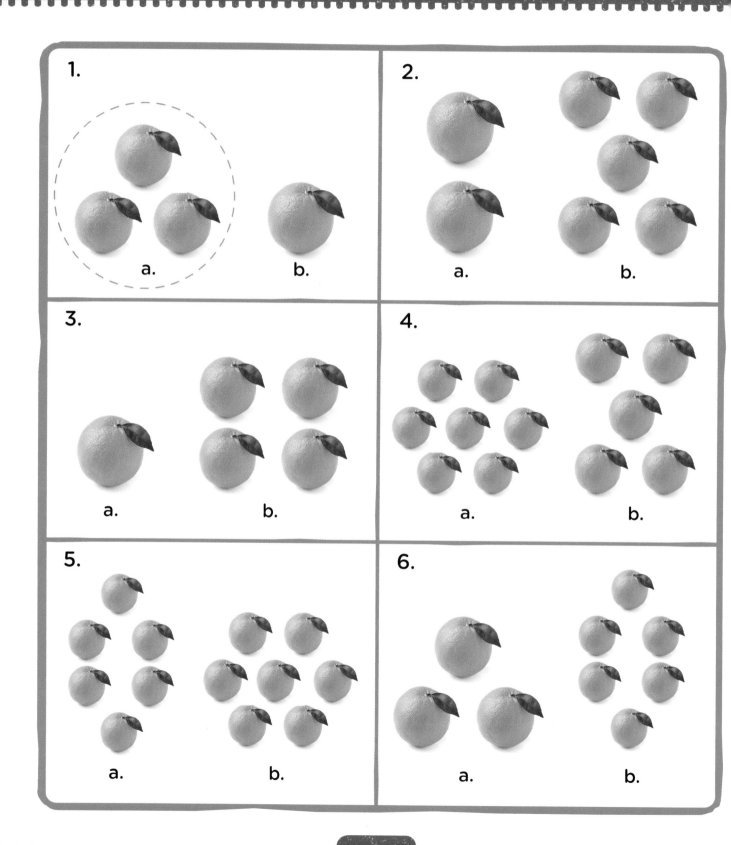

1. a. b.

2. a. b.

3. a. b.

4. a. b.

5. a. b.

6. a. b.

Busy Bees

Find the row that has **Bb** three times and circle it.

Bb	Dd	Bb
Ba	Bb	Bd
bd	Ab	Bb

Trace the letter next to each bee.

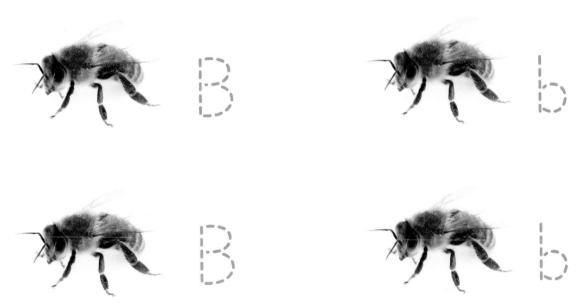

Follow the Trail

Circle the shape that comes next.

Circling C

Circle the objects that begin with the letter **C**.

Trace and write.

C c

Let's Play!

Say the names of the letters on the blocks. Then trace the letters.

Tasty Treats

Find and circle the hidden letters.

Pool Party

What will float and what will sink? Circle the objects you think will float.

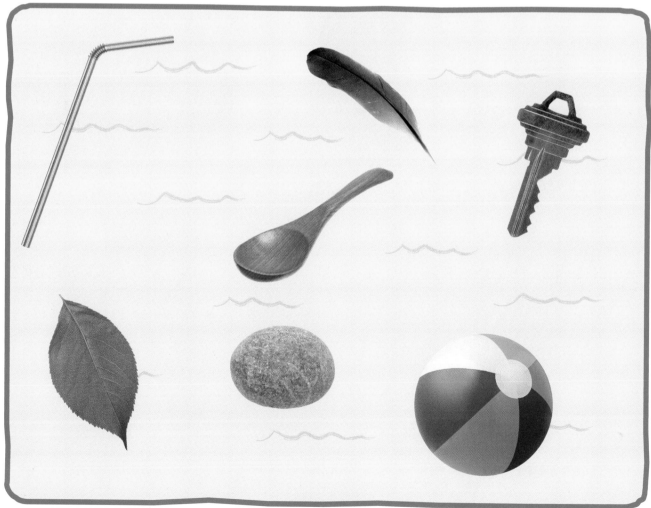

Count and Climb

Count how many objects are at the top of each ladder.
Find the equal group below and circle it.

Jobs Around Us

Draw a line to match the workers with the things they use in their jobs.

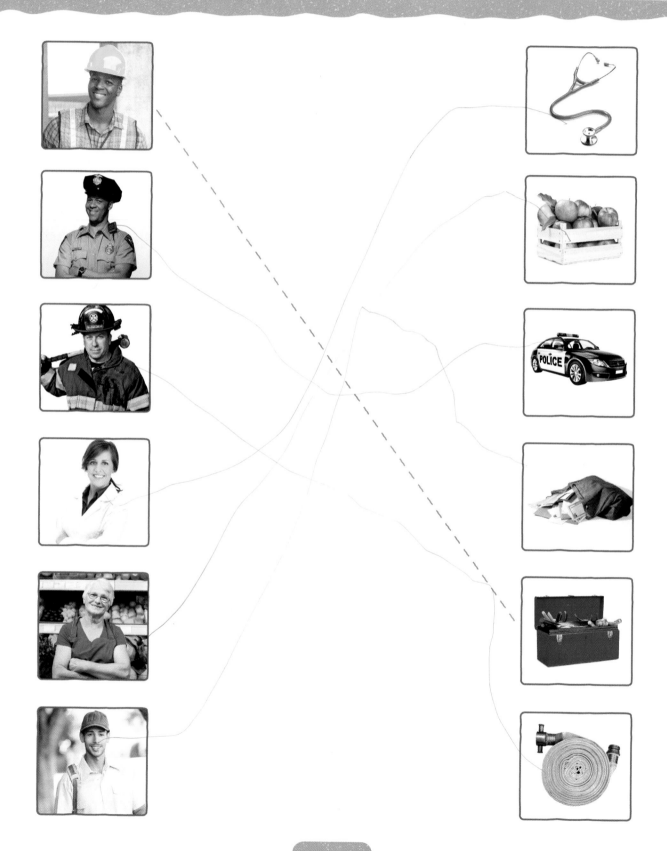

What's the Weather?

Trace the numbers on the calendar.

JUNE

SUN	MON	TUE	WED	THU	FRI	SAT
				1	2	3
4	5	6	7	8	9	10
11	12	13	14	15	16	17
18	19	20	21	22	23	24
25	26	27	28	29	30	

Count how many are on the calendar and circle the correct number.

1.

1   2   3

2.

1   2   3

3.

1   2   3

Animal Homes

Draw a line from left to right to connect each animal with its home.

Surprise Guests

There are bugs at the picnic! Count the bugs.
Then circle the number of bugs you see.

1.

| 4 | 7 | 10 |

2.

| 12 | 18 | 6 |

3.

| 1 | 9 | 5 |

4.

| 15 | 20 | 10 |

5.

| 2 | 17 | 14 |

Square Search

Find the squares, then draw a line from each to the middle.

Doggy Dad

Follow the letters **D** and **d** to help the dog find its dad.

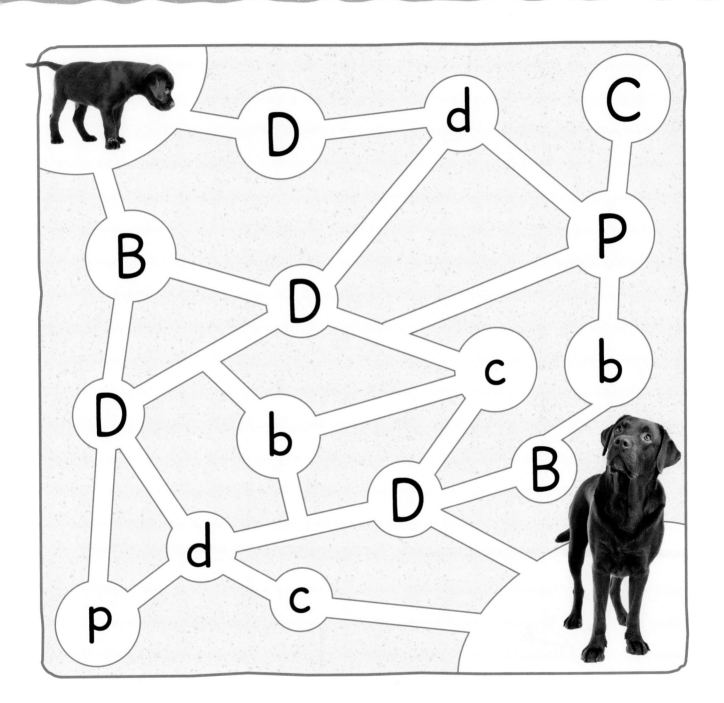

Trace and write.

Flower Garden

Circle the flowers that have matching pairs of letters.

Leap Frog

Say the name of each letter. Then write the missing letters.

1. _____ l _____ _____ _____ _____ n _____

2. _____ o _____ _____ _____ _____ q _____

3. _____ r _____ s _____ _____ _____

4. _____ _____ _____ v _____ w _____

5. _____ x _____ y _____ _____

Same Signs

Connect the matching signs.

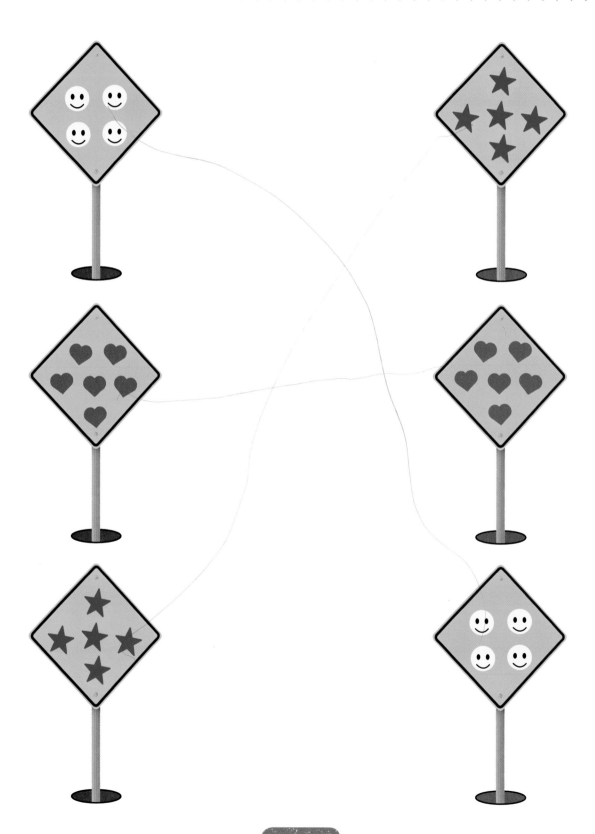

Easy E

Find the row that has **Ee** three times and circle it.

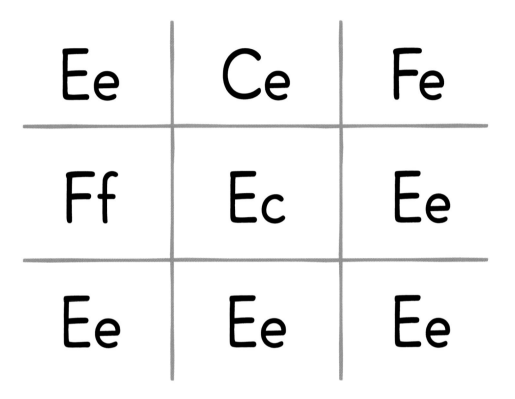

Ee	Ce	Fe
Ff	Ec	Ee
Ee	Ee	Ee

Trace the letter inside each egg.

Wonderful Water

Circle all the things that need water to live.

Fruit Match-up

Draw a line to match the pieces of cut fruit to the pieces of whole fruit.

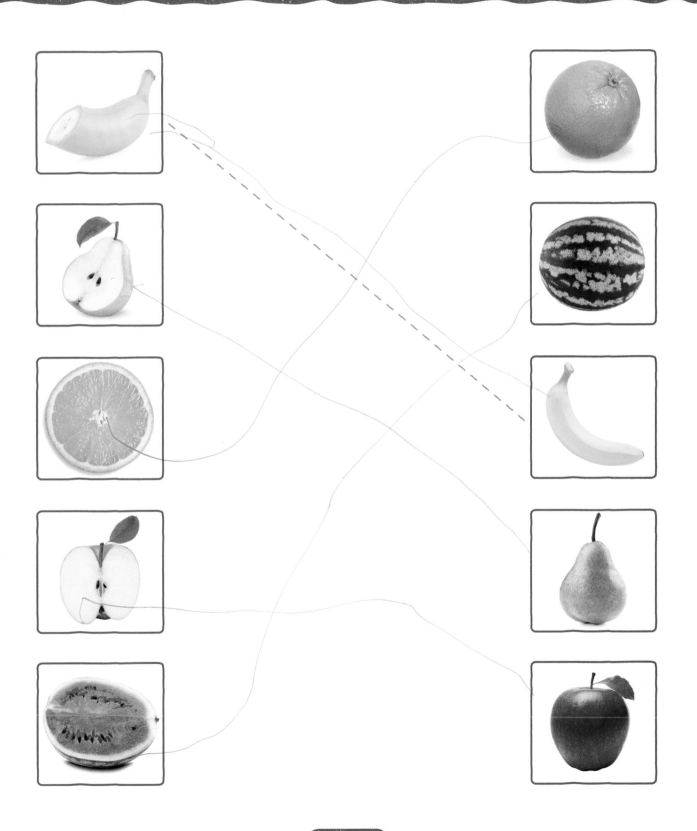

Triangle Trail

Color all the triangles to find the trail.

Finding F

Circle the objects that begin with the letter **F**.

Trace and write.

Puzzle Time

Draw a line to connect the matching letter pairs.
Your line will pass through the matching picture.

A

B

C

D

E

F

c

a

f

b

d

e

Home Run!

Trace the color circles.

Circle all the objects that are shaped like a circle.

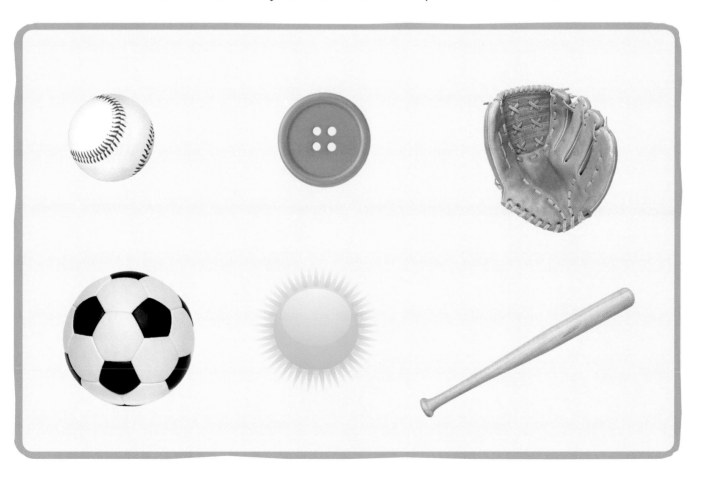

Class Birthdays

Six children in the class have birthdays this month! Draw 6 birthday cakes on the days you wish. Then fill in the missing numbers.

SEPTEMBER

SUN	MON	TUE	WED	THU	FRI	SAT
			1	2	3	4
5	6	7		9	10	11
	13		15		17	18
19		21	22	23	24	25
	27	28	29	30		

Get in Line

Trace the lines and the letters.

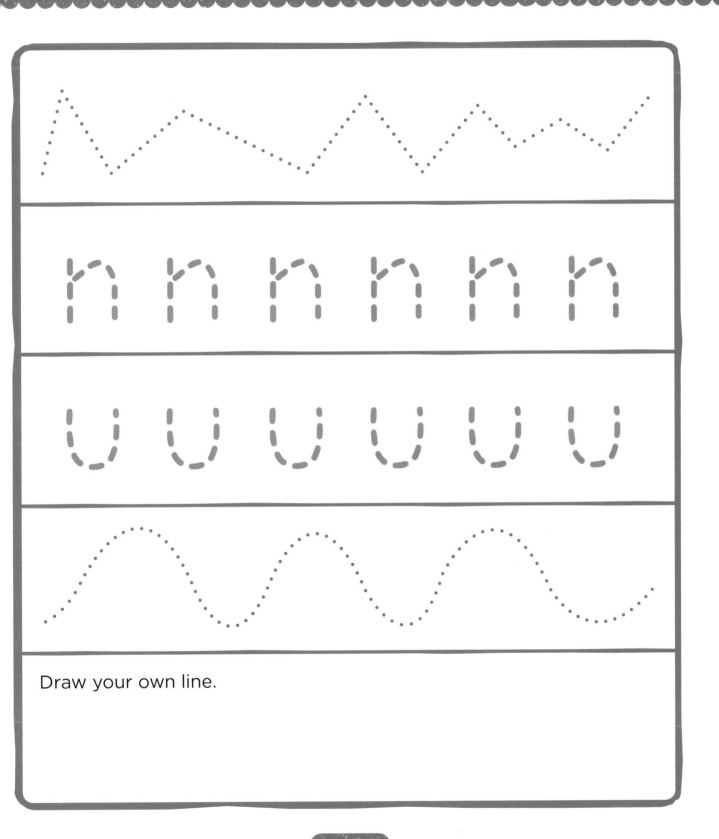

Draw your own line.

Sports Round-up

Circle the object that belongs with the first one.

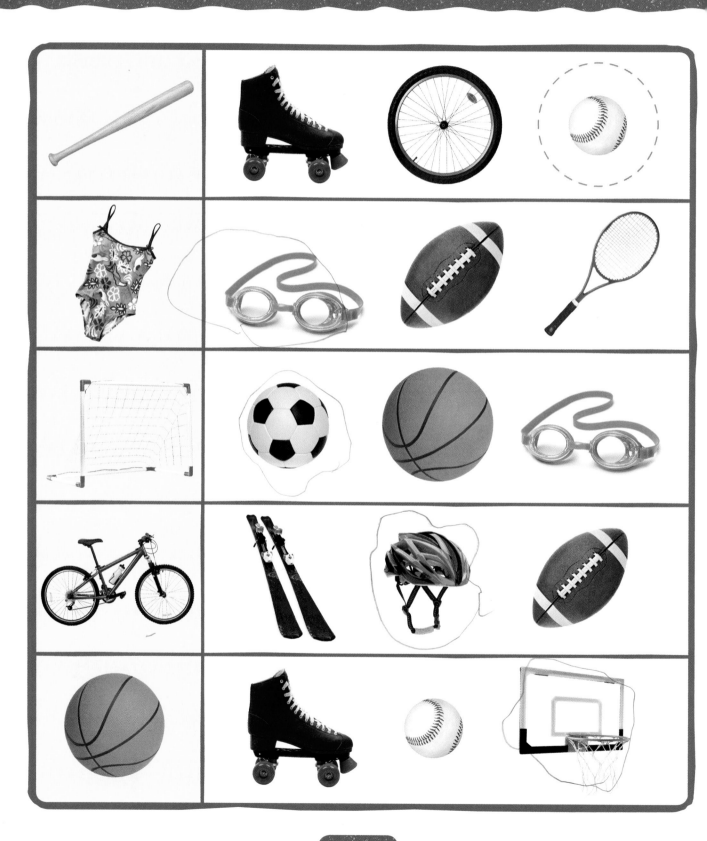

Pattern Practice

Color the pictures to finish the patterns.

1.

2.

3.

4.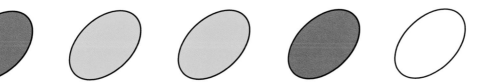

5.

Ovals Only

Find the ovals, then draw a line from each to the middle.

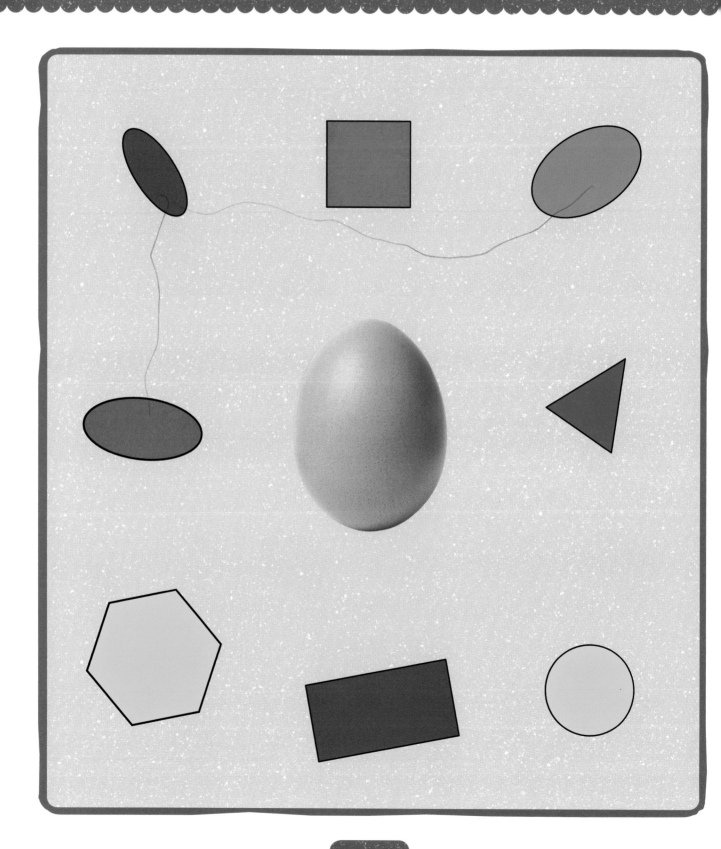

G is for Go!

Help the car find the way to the gas station.
Follow the signs with **G** or **g** to solve the maze.

Trace and write.

It's My Goal!

Trace the letters of the alphabet.

Aa Bb Cc Dd Ee Ff
Gg Hh Ii Jj Kk Ll
Mm Nn Oo Pp Qq Rr
Ss Tt Uu Vv Ww Xx
Yy Zz

Letter Match-up

Draw a line between the matching uppercase and lowercase letters.

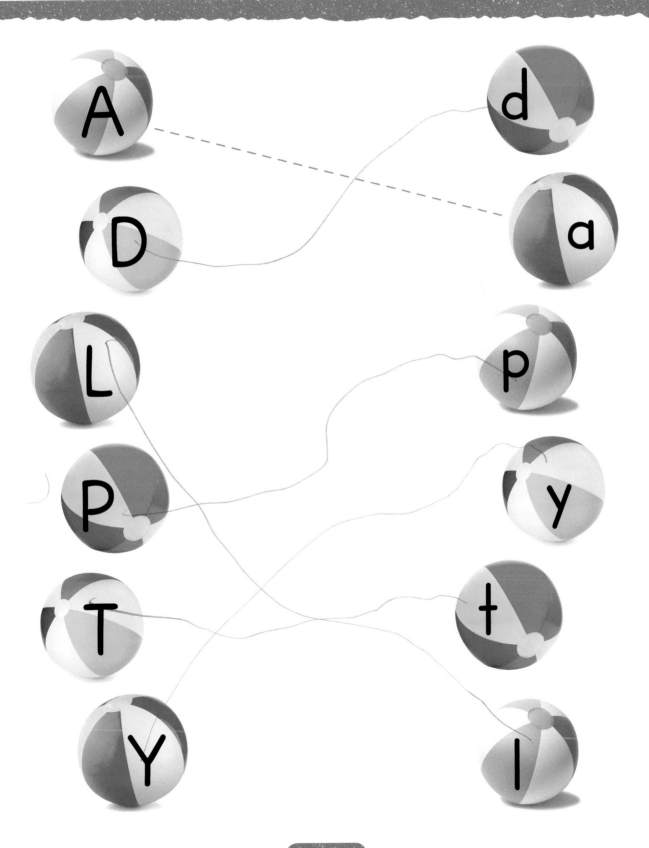

Car Count

Count the cars, then circle the number.

1.

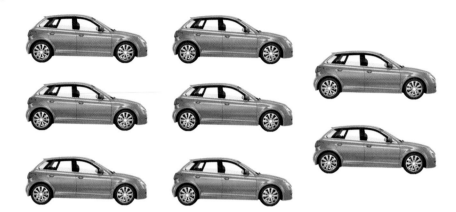 

2.

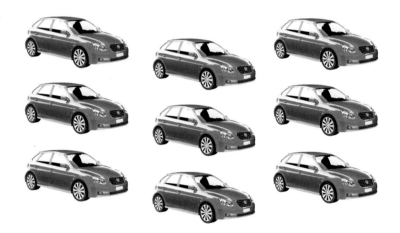 

3.

Happy Hats

Find the row that has **Hh** three times and circle it.

Hh	Hh	Ih
Ed	Hh	Hh
Hh	Hh	Hb

Trace the letter on each hat.

Take Me Out to the Ball Game!

Write the word to finish each sentence. Draw a line to the matching picture.

You use your eyes to **see**.

You use your ears to **hear**.

You use your mouth to **taste**.

You use your nose to **smell**.

You use your hands to **touch** and feel.

1. The batter feels the hard bat with his ___hands___ .

2. The girl tastes the hot dog with her _____ .

3. The man watches the game with his _____ .

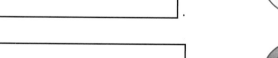

4. The player uses his _____ to hear the whistle blow.

5. The boy smells the popcorn with his _____ .

The Golden Rule

Good citizens help others. Good citizens follow the rules. Look at each pair of pictures. Circle the picture that shows someone being a good citizen.

1.

2.

Hidden Trails

Follow the color code to find the hidden trails.

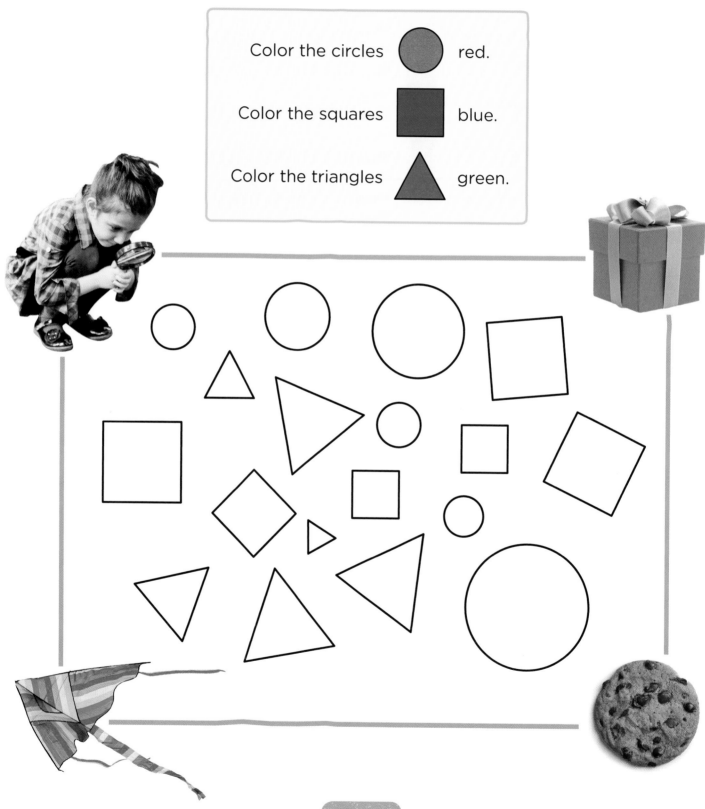

Color the circles ⬤ red.

Color the squares ⬛ blue.

Color the triangles 🔺 green.

I Love I

Circle the objects that begin with the letter **i**.

Trace and write.

Keeping Fit

Circle all the pictures that show a child doing something healthy.

Camp Size 'Em Up

Circle the picture in each row that is the same size as the first.

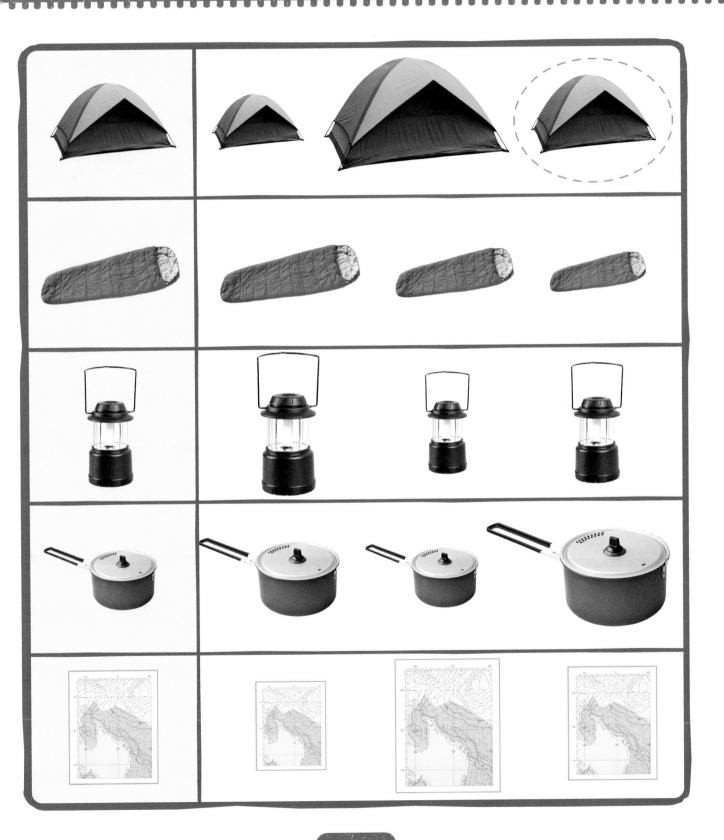

What's First

Circle the picture that shows what happens first in each row.

1.

2.

Camping Time

Draw a line from the sun to each thing that happens during the day.
Then draw a line from the moon to each thing that happens at night.

Animal Sounds

Look at the animals. Say their names.
Then write the lowercase letter that begins each animal name.

1.

_____ c

2.

_____

3.

_____

4.

_____

5.

_____

6.

_____

Vacation Time

Fill in or trace the numbers on the calendar.

APRIL

SUN	MON	TUE	WED	THU	FRI	SAT
						1
	3	4		6	7	8
9	10	11	12	13	14	15
16	17	18	19	20	21	22
23/30	24	25	26	27	28	29

The shaded days show vacation time! Count the number of vacation days and write the number in the box below.

Space Case

Circle the sentence if the words are separated by spaces.
If there are no spaces, cross it out.

Words are always
separated by spaces.

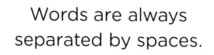

Thecarcango.

 Mom has a hat.

The car needs some gas.

 Thehatisontheelephant.

 Dadhasafish.

 The ants are on the apple.

Take a Hike

Help the campers find their tent. Follow the path and circle the letter that shows the beginning sound for each picture.

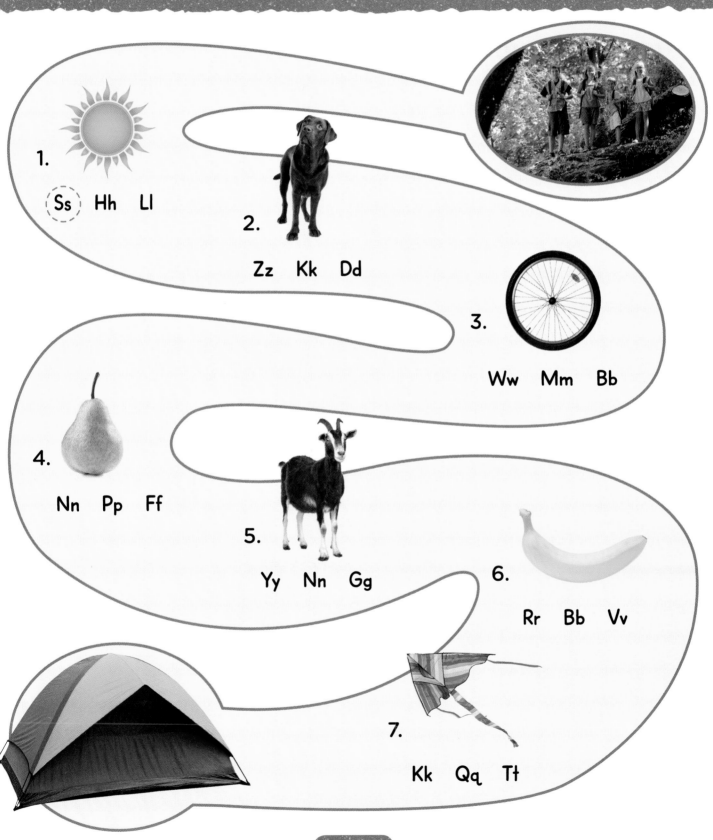

1. Ss Hh Ll

2. Zz Kk Dd

3. Ww Mm Bb

4. Nn Pp Ff

5. Yy Nn Gg

6. Rr Bb Vv

7. Kk Qq Tt

Camping is Cool

Circle the picture that has the same beginning sound as the first one.

Rectangles All Around

Find the rectangles, then draw a line from each to the middle.

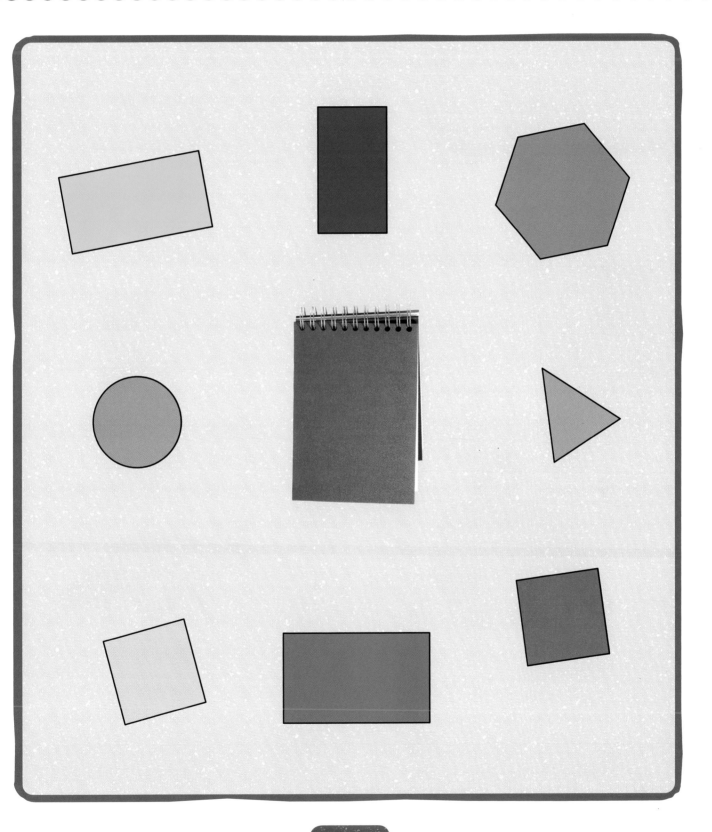

Jump for J

Circle the pictures whose names start with **J**.

Trace and write.

J J

Terrific Trees

Read the story. Look at the pictures. Then draw a picture in the box.

Trees give us food.

Trees shade us from the sun.

Trees are homes to birds.

Trees have so much to give!

Dot to Dot

Count from **1** to **10** to connect the dots.

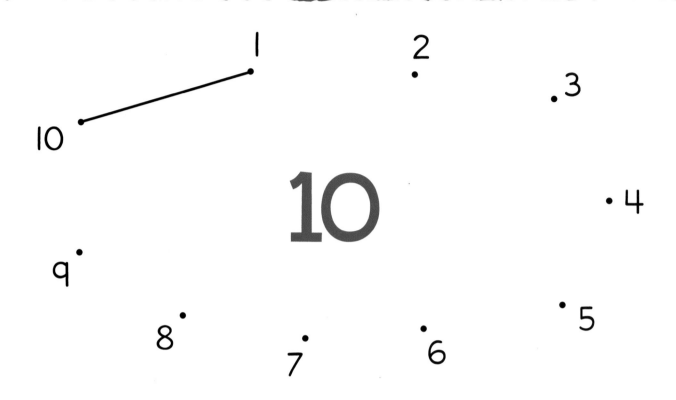

Write the number **10** ten times.

The Right Kite

Say the name of each picture. Circle the row
of pictures whose names begin with **K**.

Circle the kites with the letters **Kk**.

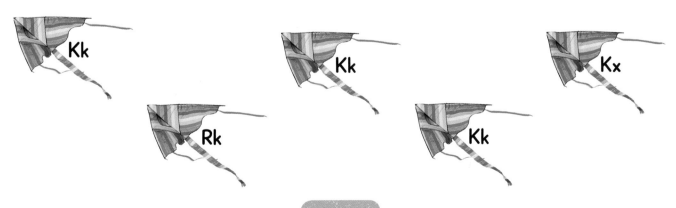

Family Time

Draw a line to match each word to a picture.

Mom

Dad

Kids

Grandma

Grandpa

Family

Trail of Ten

Draw 10 circles along the trail.

Looking for L Words

Circle the objects that begin with the letter **L**.

Trace and write.

Triangle Time!

Trace and color the triangles.

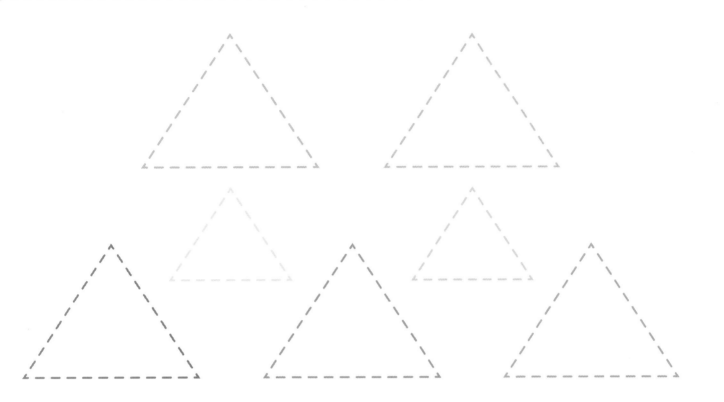

Circle all the objects that are shaped like a triangle.

Panda Parade

Each picture in the box completes the pattern in a row of pandas.
Find the picture that completes each pattern and write the letter on the line.

a)   b)   c)   d)

1. ____

2. ____

3. ____

4. ____

Puzzle Page

Draw a line to connect each matching letter pair. Then draw a line from the letter to the picture whose name begins with that letter.

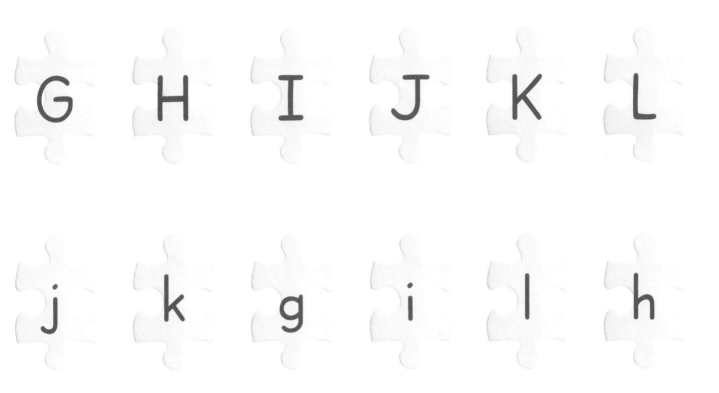

G H I J K L

j k g i l h

Zany Zoo

Say the name of each animal. Draw a line to the letter
that shows the beginning sound for the animal.

1.

2.

3.

4.

5.

Ll   Ff   Zz   Kk   Gg

6.

7.

8.

9.

10.

Mm   Bb   Ss   Tt   Hh

Find Your Way

Trace the path to each child's favorite animal.

After-School Sports

Fill in the missing numbers on the calendar.

OCTOBER

SUN	MON	TUE	WED	THU	FRI	SAT
		2 ⚽		4 ⚽	5 🧤	
7		9 ⚽	10	11 ⚽	🧤	13
14	15	16 ⚽	17	18 ⚽	19 🧤	20
21	22	23 ⚽	24	25 ⚽	26 🧤	27
28	29	30	31			

Count how many are on the calendar and circle the correct number.

2   3   4   5

6   7   8   9

Word Slide

Blend the letters, then trace or write the word.

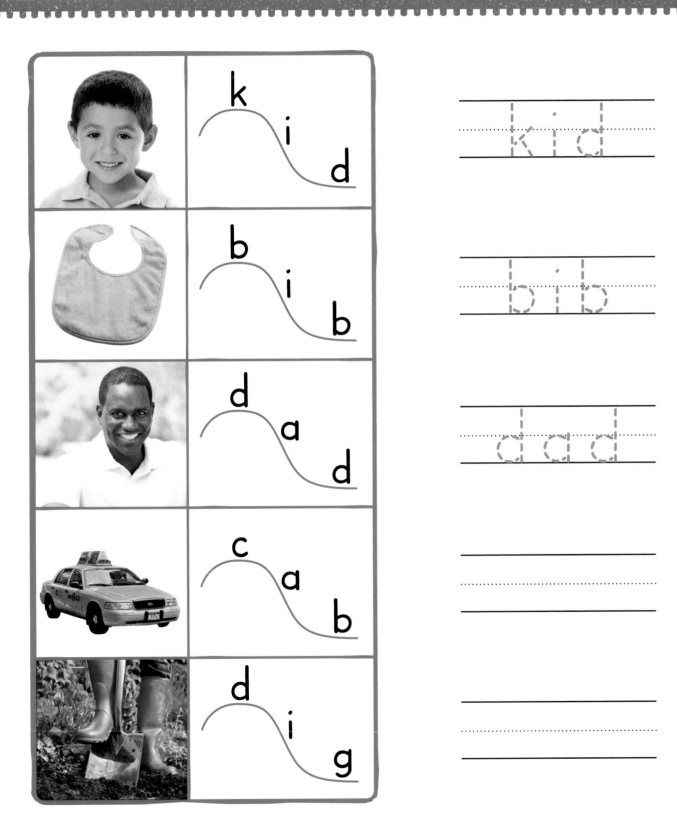

k i d		kid
b i b		bib
d a d		dad
c a b		
d i g		

Amazing Animals

Draw a line to match each baby animal to its parent.

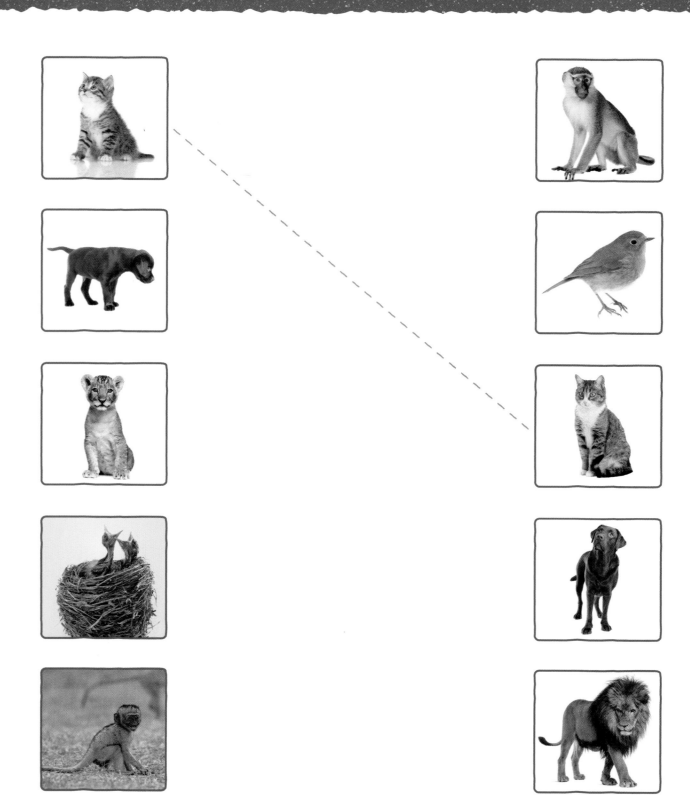

Where Are They?

Look at the map. Answer the questions.

1. Which is closest to the flamingo ?   a)    b)

2. Which is to the left of the lion  ?   a)   b)

3. Which is the farthest from the giraffe ?   a)   b)

Which Is Longer?

Find the longer one in each pair.

LONGER

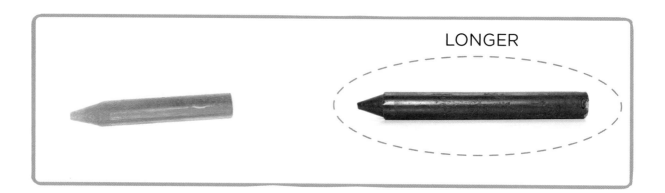

1. a)

    b)

2. a)

    b)

3. a)

    b)

4. a)  b)

Monkey in the Middle

Follow the letters **M** and **m** to the monkey in the middle of the maze.

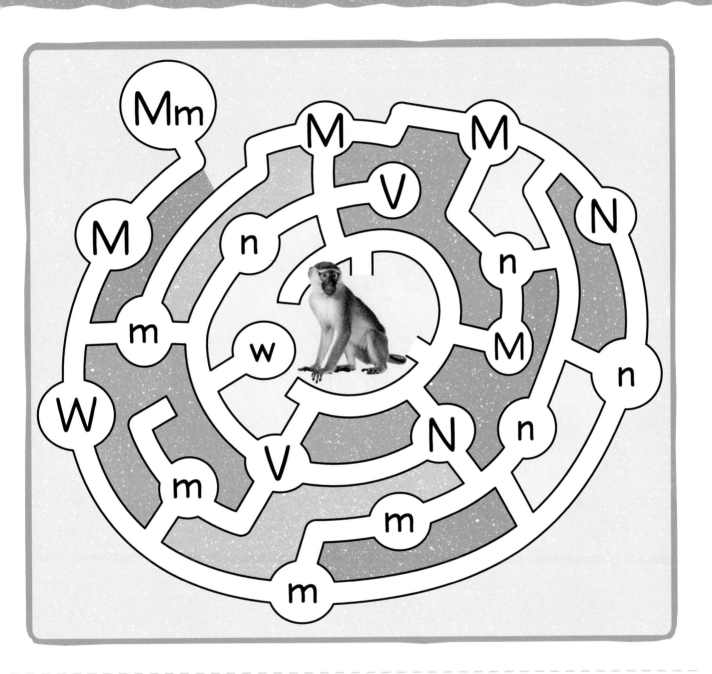

Trace and write.

Mm

Fun in the Sun

Circle the objects in each row that you would take to the beach.
Cross out the objects that you would not take.

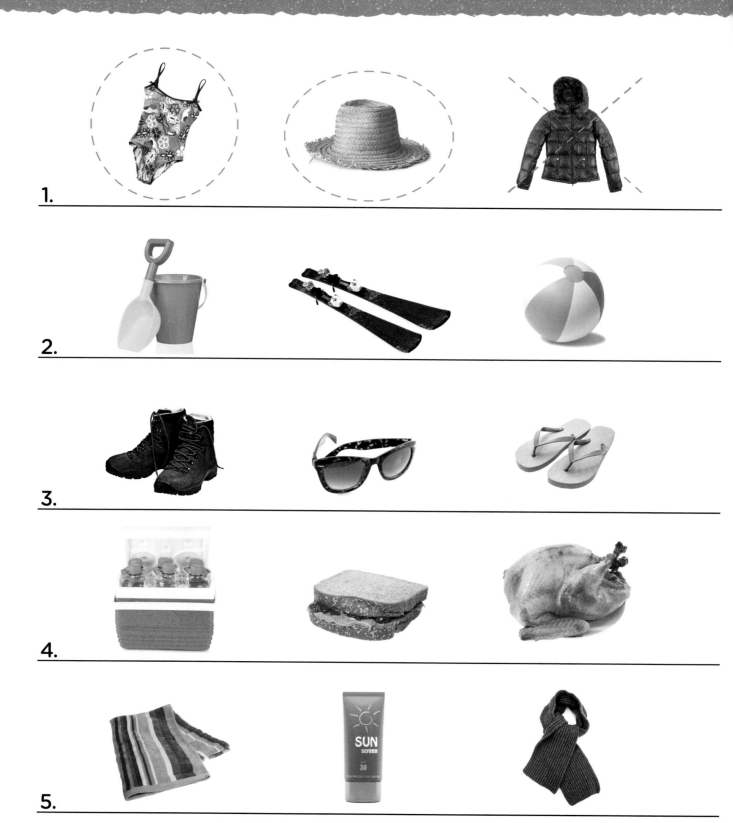

1.

2.

3.

4.

5.

Car Count

Count the cars. Trace or write the number.

1.

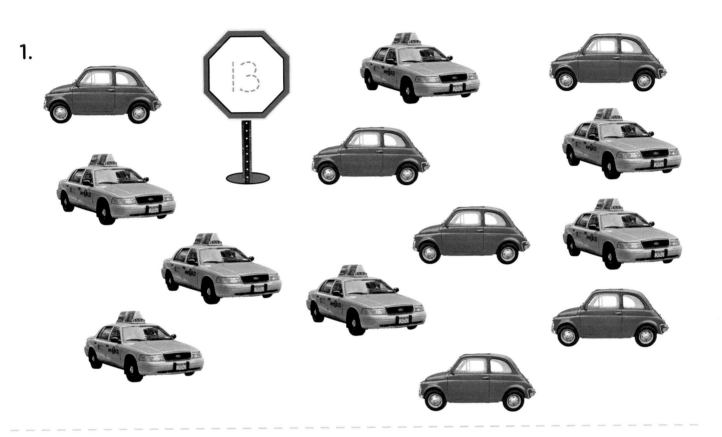

2.

Nuts about N

Find the row that has **Nn** three times and circle it.

Kn	Mn	Nn
Nu	Nn	Nn
Nn	Nm	Nw

Trace the letter on each nut.

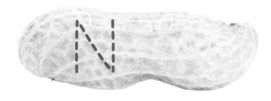

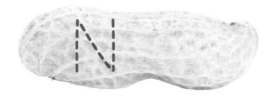

Boxes and Boxes

Trace and color the squares and rectangles.

Circle all the objects that are shaped like a square.
Cross out all the objects that are shaped like a rectangle.

Down by the Sea

Say the name of each picture. Draw a line
to match each word to a rhyming word.

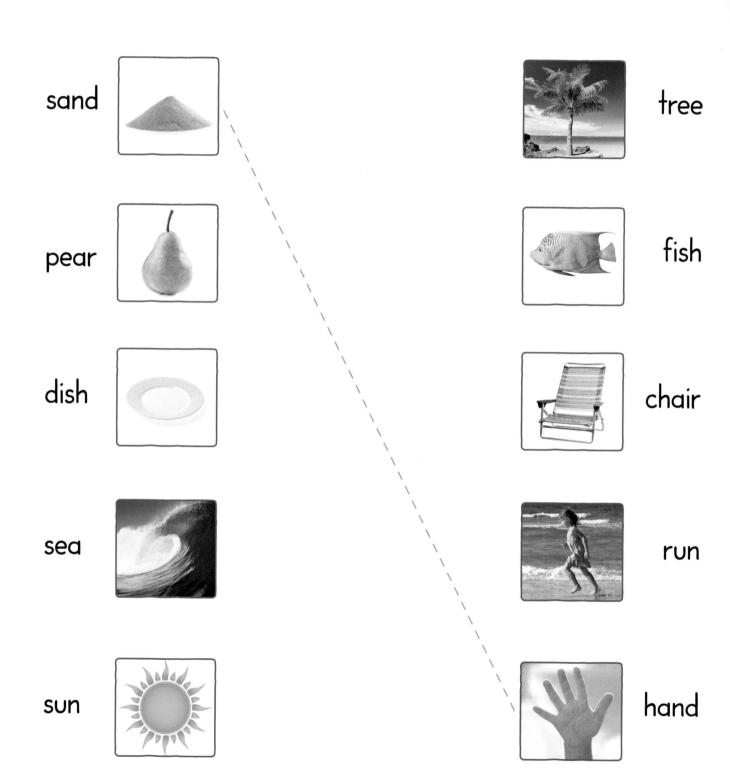

sand

pear

dish

sea

sun

tree

fish

chair

run

hand

Pattern Path

Fill in the missing shapes along each row.

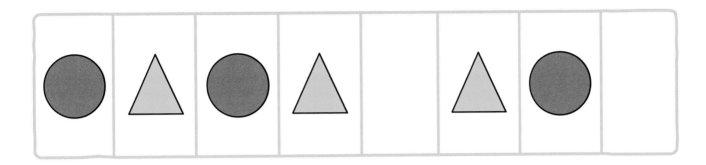

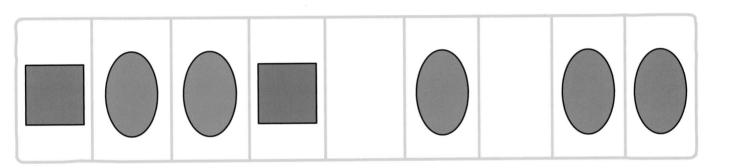

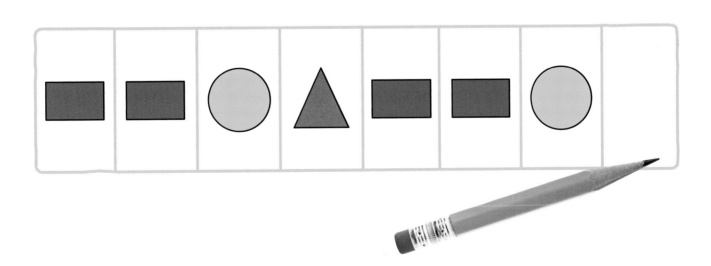

Know about O

Circle the objects that begin with the letter **O**.

Trace and write.

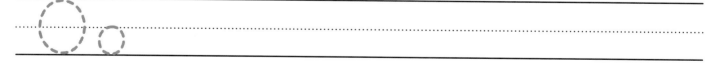

Food at the Fair

Trace the uppercase letters. Then fill in the missing letters.

1.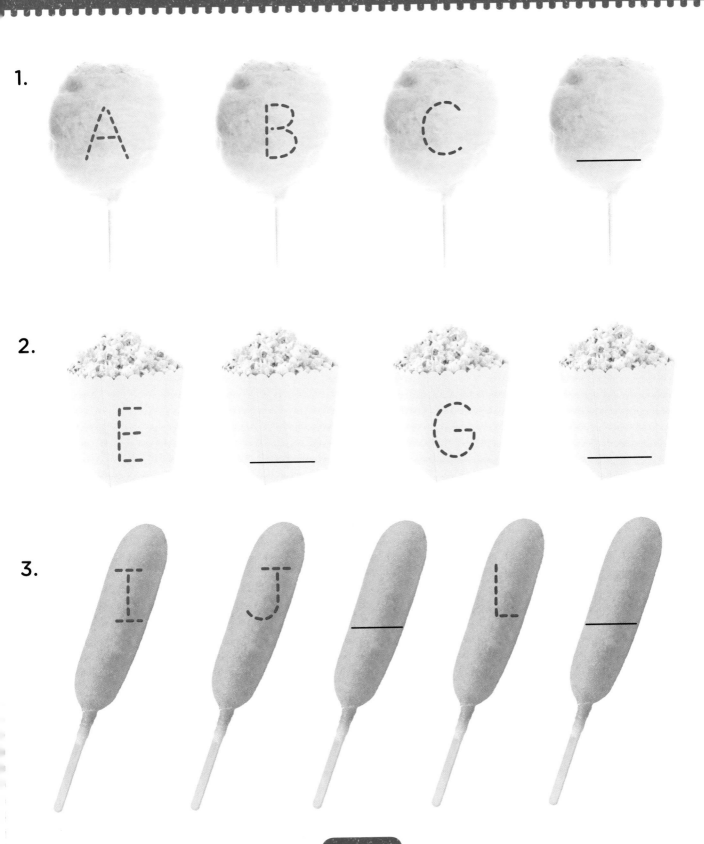

A B C ___

2. E ___ G ___

3. I J ___ L ___

Cotton Candy Is Dandy

Trace the lowercase letters. Then fill in the missing letters.

1. n   o   ____   q

2. r   ____   ____   u

3. ____   w   x   ____   z

Speak Up!

You can make up what the characters are saying in each picture.
Have an adult write it in the bubbles for you.

Blowing in the Wind

Circle all of the things that can fly in the sky.

Beach Combers

There are many animals at the beach! Draw a cloud around the animals that can fly. Draw waves under the animals that can swim.

Calendar Code

Fill in the missing numbers on the calendar. Then follow the directions below.

NOVEMBER

SUN	MON	TUE	WED	THU	FRI	SAT
			1	2		4
5	6		8	9	10	
12	13	14		16	17	18
19	20	21	22	23	24	25
26	27	28	29	30		

Circle the numbers on November **11**, **12**, and **13**.

Draw a ☁ on November **4**, **5**, **6**, **7**, and **8**.

Draw a ☀ on November **9** and **10**.

Put an **X** on November **1** and **15**.

Color November **3** blue.

Word Match

Circle the matching letters in each row.

l	T	l	i
a	a	d	c
it	ti	it	jt
is	js	iz	is
to	to	ta	fo

Beach Town

Look at the map. Circle the answers to each question.

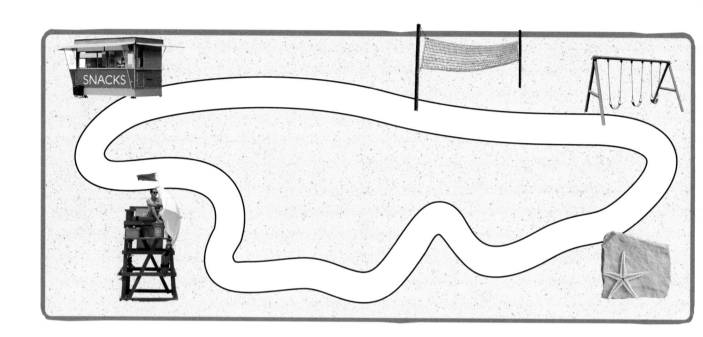

1. Pam is at the . She wants to go to the .
   What will she pass along the way?

   a)   b)   c)

2. Mary is riding her bike on the path. She passes the
   and then the . What direction is she going?

   a) ↑   b) ↓   c) →   d) ←

3. What is farthest from the ?

   a)    b)    c)

Luggage Lineup

Follow the directions.

Write the number that comes next.

1.  6 7 8

2.  15 16 ☐

3. 21 22 ☐

4. 28 29 ☐

5. 12 13 ☐

6. 9 10 ☐

Write the number that comes between.

7.  1 2 3

8.  22 ☐ 24

9. 14 ☐ 16

10. 18 ☐ 20

11.  24 ☐ 26

12. 8 ☐ 10

Write the number that comes before.

13.  3 4 5

14. ☐ 7 8

15.  ☐ 18 19

16. ☐ 28 29

17.  ☐ 16 17

18. ☐ 11 12

Which Is Shorter?

Circle the shorter one in each pair.

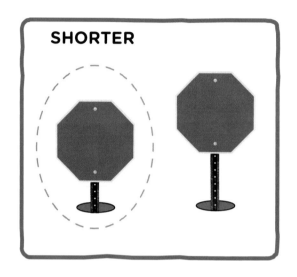

SHORTER

1.

a)

b)

2.

a)

b)

3.

a)

b)

4.

a)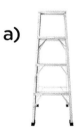

b)

Pigpen P

Follow the pictures whose names start with **P** to solve the maze.

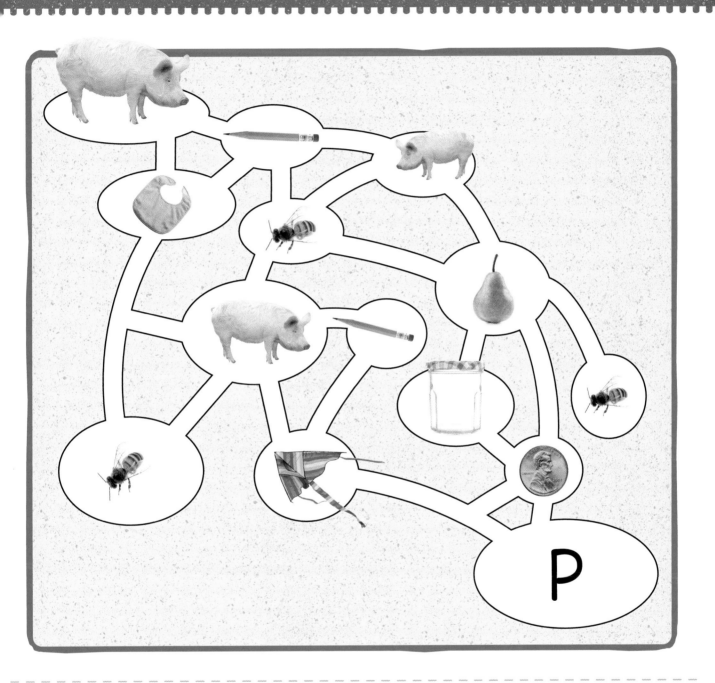

Trace and write.

Hello, Hawaii!

Count these objects that you might find in Hawaii.
Write the number of objects on each line.

1.  ____ 7

2. ____

3. ____

4. ____

5. ____

6. ____

Silly Seals!

Count the seals in each group. Write the number of seals on each line.

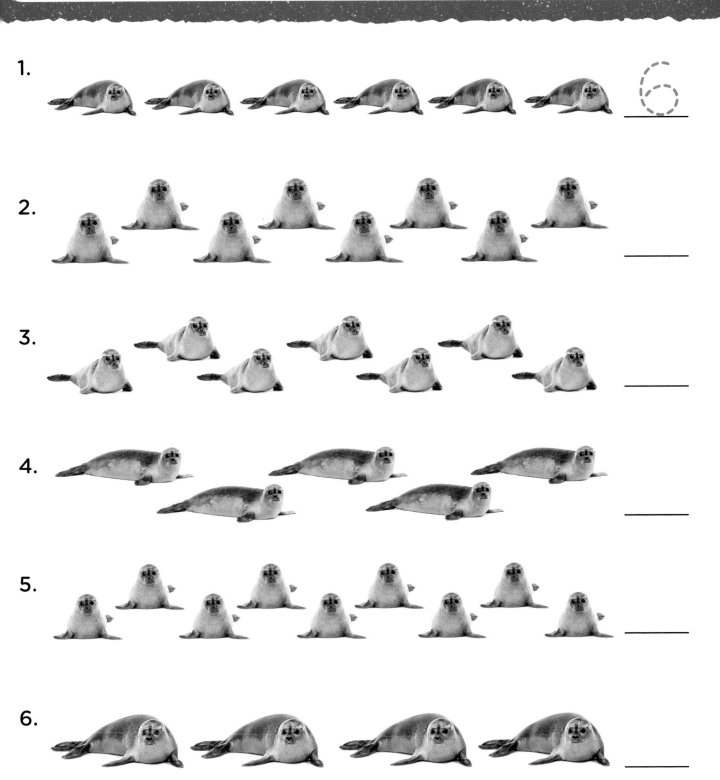

1. _6_

2. _____

3. _____

4. _____

5. _____

6. _____

High Number Highway

Count the dots on each sign, then trace and write the totals.

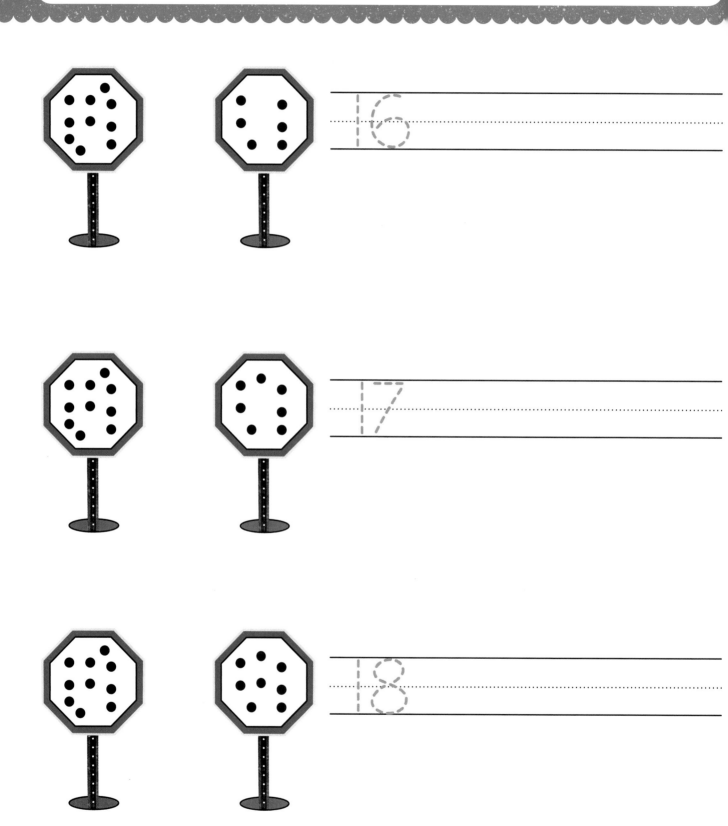

Queen of the Q

Find the row that has **Qq** three times and circle it.

Qp	Qq	Oq
Qq	Qq	Qq
Oj	Qg	Qq

Trace the letters **Qq**.

Feathers, Fur, or Scales?

Put the animals in groups.

Draw a ⭕ around the animals that have feathers.

Draw a ⬜ around the animals that have fur.

Draw a △ around the animals that have scales.

Super Sun!

Draw a line to match each uppercase letter to its lowercase letter.

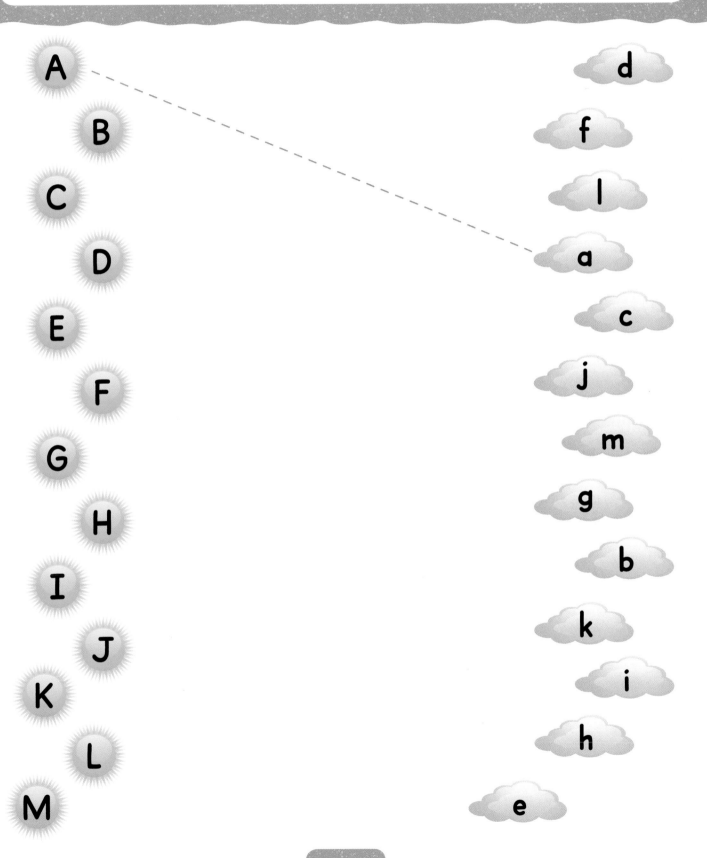

Rooting for R

Circle the objects that begin with the letter **R**.

Trace and write.

R r

Lunch Letters

Draw a line to match each uppercase letter to its lowercase letter.

Number Match

Circle the number on each ladder that matches the number at the top.

16

17

18

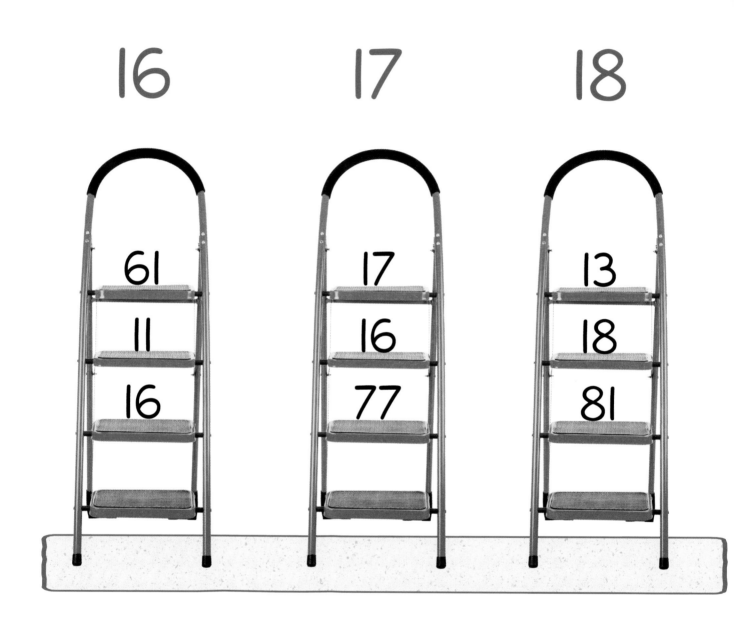

16	17	18
61	17	13
11	16	18
16	77	81

Trace and write the numbers.

16 17 18

Puzzle Page

Cross out the object or letter that doesn't belong in each group.

School Supplies

Trace the lowercase letters. Then fill in the missing letters.

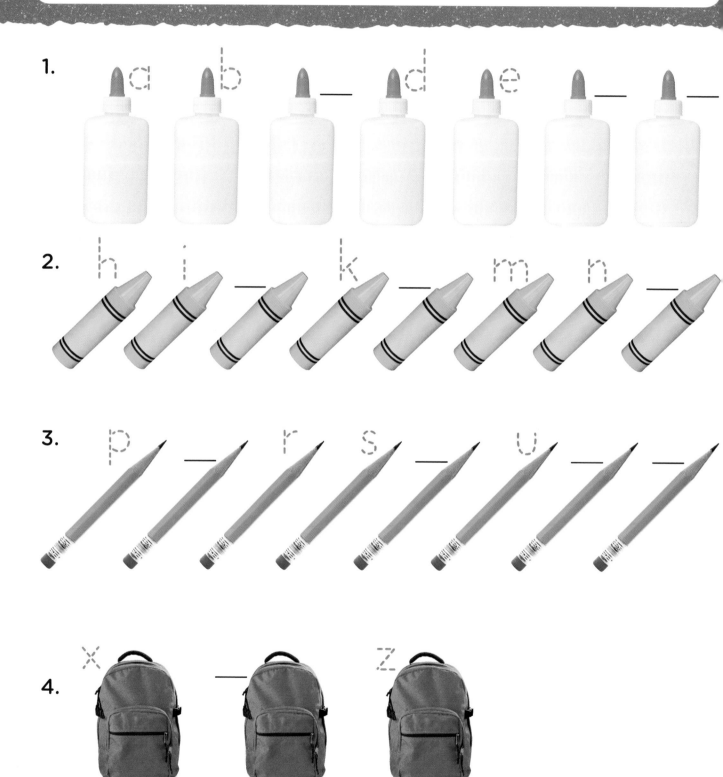

1. a b ___ d e ___ ___

2. h i ___ k ___ m n ___

3. p ___ r s ___ u ___ ___

4. x ___ z

Yum! Yum!

Count the ice cream scoops. Write the number of scoops under each cone.
Then circle the bigger number.

1. ___2___   ___1___

2. _____   _____

3. _____   _____

4. _____   _____

Wacky Weeks

Complete the pattern for each week.

FEBRUARY

SUN	MON	TUE	WED	THU	FRI	SAT
1 ✗	2 ●	3 ✗	4 ●	5 ✗	6 ●	7
8 ♥	9 ★	10 ★	11 ♥	12 ★	13 ★	14
15 △	16 ▽	17 △	18 ▽	19 △	20 ▽	21
22 ●	23 ■	24 △	25 ●	26 ■	27 △	28

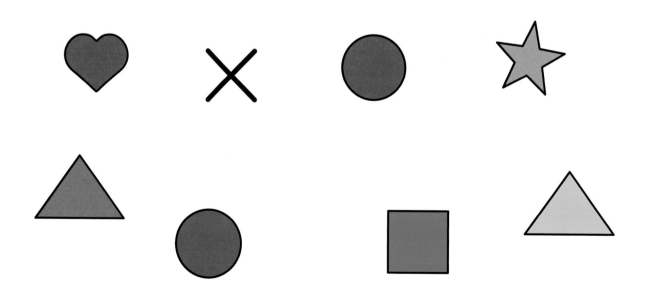

Know Your Name

Write the first letter of each child's name.

1. Sam

S

2. Kami

K

3. Tom

4. Now write the first letter of your own name.

5. Have an adult write your name. Then copy it on the line.

Flower Power

Fill in the missing numbers.

1 _ _ 4 _

_ 7 _ _ _

11 _ _ _ 15

_ _ 18 _ _

_ 22 _ _ _

_ _ 28 _ 30

Friendly Fish

Circle each fish with the color that is written below the fish.

red

blue

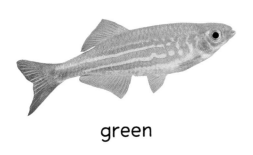

green

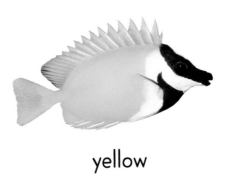

yellow

orange

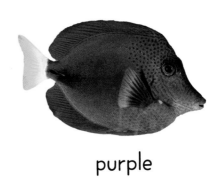

purple

I Want More!

Find the group with more.

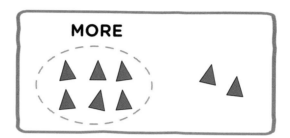
1.

a)

b)

2.

a)

b)

3.

a)

b)

4.

a)

b)

Rhyme Time

Say the name of each picture. Trace the word.
Then draw a picture of something that rhymes with it.

 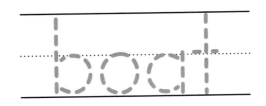

 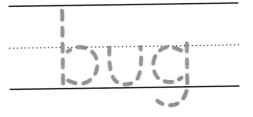

Sandy Words

The children are writing words in the sand. Trace the words.
Then write the words a second time.

pail

hat

sun

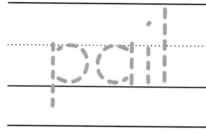

wave

crab

Road Racers

Fill in the missing numbers as you count the race cars.

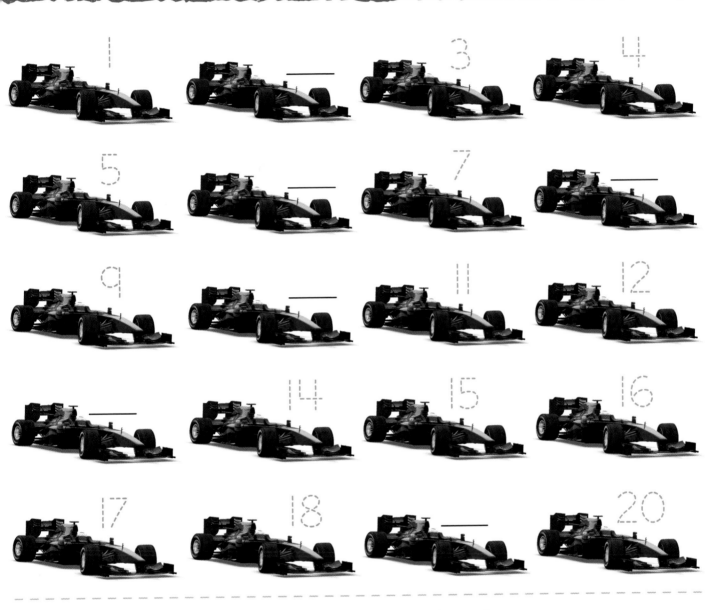

Trace and write the number **19**.

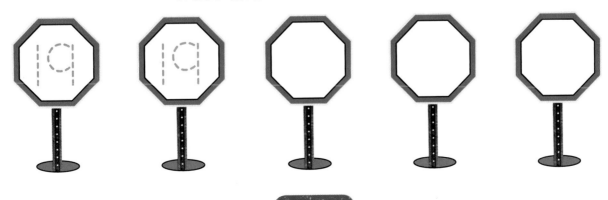

Time for T

Say the name of each picture. Circle the row of three pictures whose names begin with **T**.

Circle the turtles with the letters **Tt**.

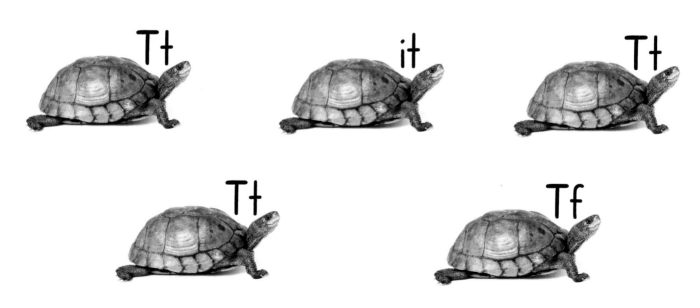

Petting Zoo

Draw a line to match each adult animal to its baby.

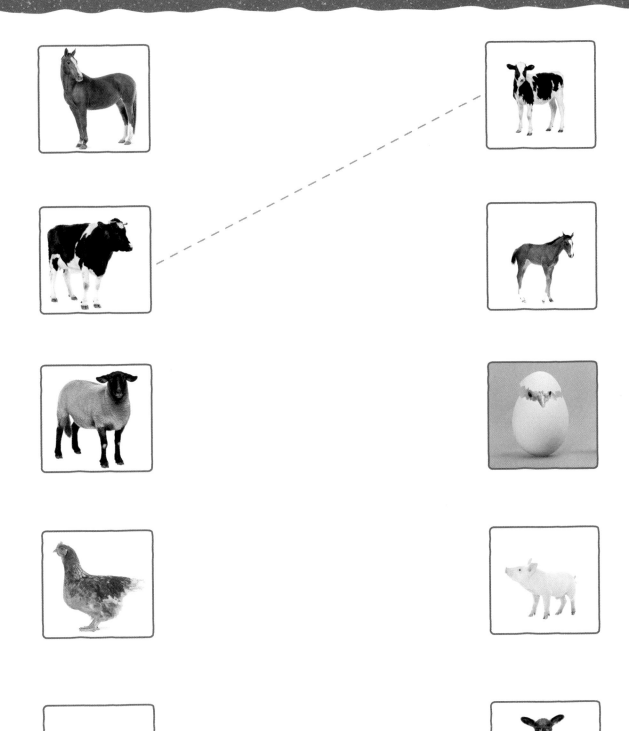

Common Senses

Circle the word that best describes each item.

1.

a) hard   (b) soft)   c) hot

2.

a) sour   b) cold   c) sweet

3.

a) bright   b) dark   c) spicy

4.

a) quiet   b) loud   c) rough

5.

a) salty   b) tart   c) pretty

Box of Rocks

Count the number of stones in each box.
Then add one stone and write the total on the line.

1.

3   +   1   = __4__

2.

4   +   1   = _____

3.

5   +   1   = _____

Unique U

Circle the objects that begin with the letter **U**.

Trace and write.

A Good Citizen

Use the words in the word box to finish the sentence.

| Earth | manners | respect | rules |

1. A good citizen follows the 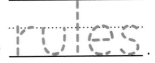 .

2. A good citizen treats others with _____ .

3. A good citizen takes care of _____ .

4. A good citizen uses good _____ .

Beach Camp

Count the number of shells in each group. Then circle the number that is closest to the number of shells.

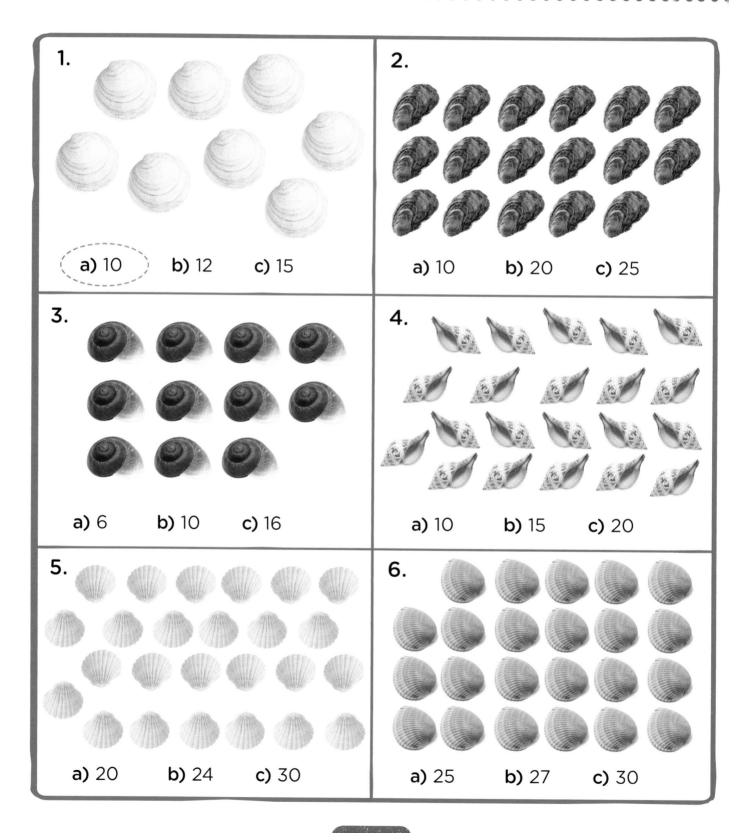

1.

a) 10   b) 12   c) 15

2.

a) 10   b) 20   c) 25

3.

a) 6   b) 10   c) 16

4.

a) 10   b) 15   c) 20

5.

a) 20   b) 24   c) 30

6.

a) 25   b) 27   c) 30

Story Out of Order

Number the pictures **1** to **4** to show the order of events.

Make up a title for the story and ask an adult to write it down.

Nature Camp

Say the name of each picture. Trace the word. Then write the word.

tree

tent

pot

map

Do-Re-Me

At Camp Melody, campers are taught to play musical instruments.
Look at the graph to see how many campers play each instrument.

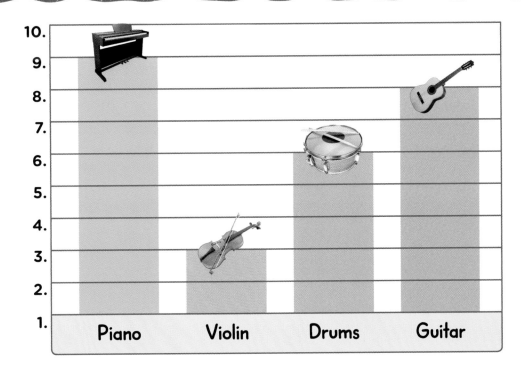

1. How many more campers
play the than the ?

a) 3   b) 5   c) 10

2. Which instrument is played by
the least number of campers?

a)   b)   c)

3. Which instrument is played by
the most number of campers?

a)   b)   c)

4. Draw a picture of an instrument
you would like to play.

Book Buddies

The calendar shows how many books Sam, Kim, and Tom read this month.

JANUARY

SUN	MON	TUE	WED	THU	FRI	SAT
			1	2 Sam	3	4
5 Kim	6	7	8	9	10 Tom	11
12	13	14 Sam	15	16	17	18
19 Kim	20	21	22	23	24	25
26	27	28	29	30 Sam	31	

Count the books for each person and write the number below.
Then add the numbers to show how many books they read in total.

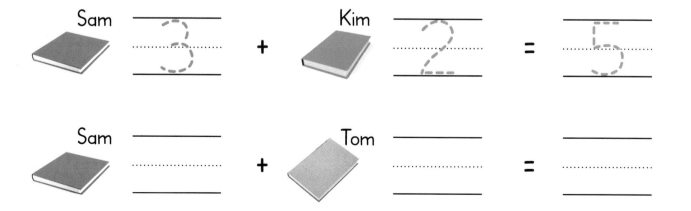

Sam ___ 3 ___ + Kim ___ 2 ___ = ___ 5 ___

Sam _____ + Tom _____ = _____

Word Find

Circle the matching word in each row.

am	am an om
to	tq fo to
my	ny my mm
me	ne my me
and	and am add

Go Team!

Read the words on the megaphones. Draw lines
to match the words that rhyme.

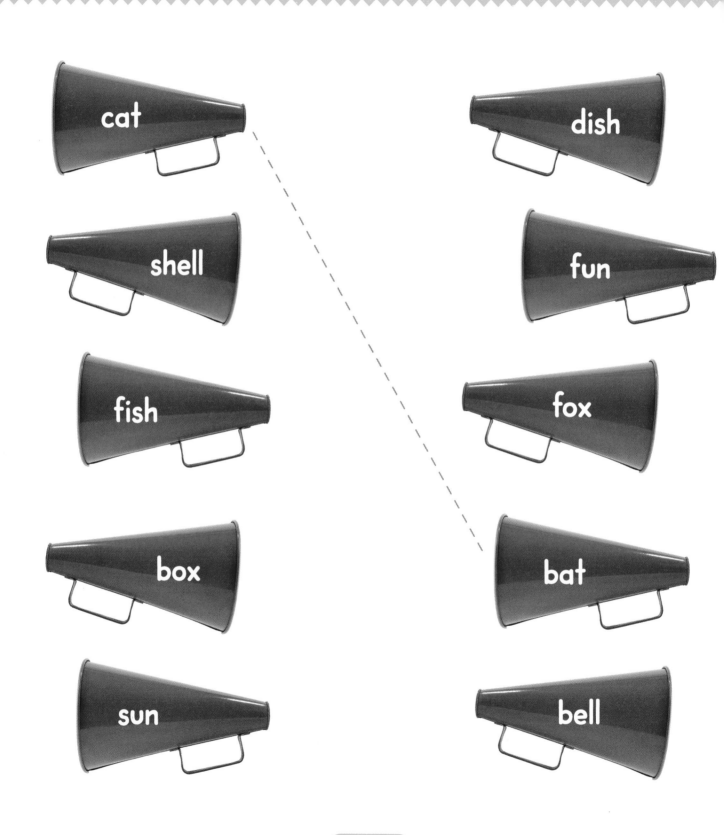

cat

dish

shell

fun

fish

fox

box

bat

sun

bell

Wonderful Wheels

Read the story.

Circle the picture that answers each question.

1. What did 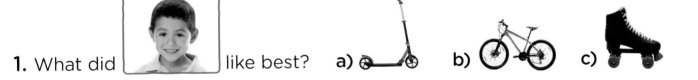 like best? a) b) c)

2. Who liked to ride the 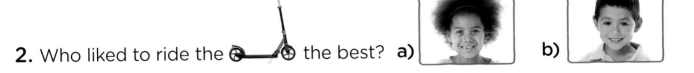 the best? a) b)

Money in the Middle

Find the coins, then draw a line from each to the middle.

Super Seasons

Look at the pictures. Write the name of the season that matches each tree.
Use the words in the box to label each picture.

winter   spring   summer   fall

1. _winter_

2. _____

3. _____

4. _____

Antsy Addition

Add the ants, then write the total.

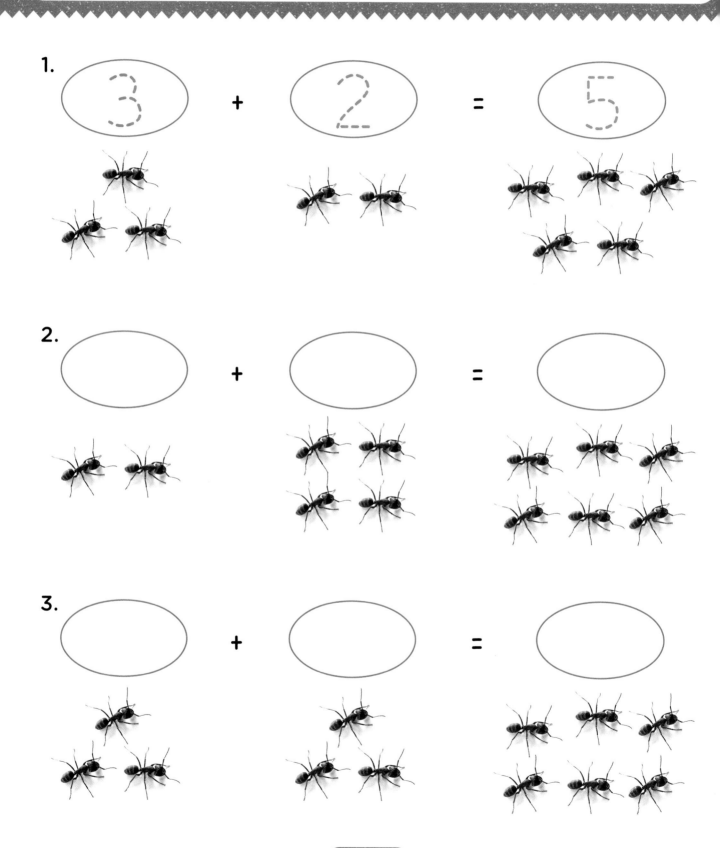

1. (3) + (2) = (5)

2. (   ) + (   ) = (   )

3. (   ) + (   ) = (   )

Wagon Wheels

Find the row that has **Ww** three times and circle it.

Ww	Vw	Wv
Ww	WW	Xw
Ww	Ww	Wy

Trace the letters **Ww** around the wagon.

Ww   Ww

Ww   Ww

Camp Calendar

Look at the calendar. Then answer the questions.

AUGUST

SUN	MON	TUE	WED	THU	FRI	SAT
1	2	3	4	5	6	7
8 Campers Arrive	9	10	11 Trip to Lake	12	13	14 Hayride
15	16	17 Horseback Riding	18	19 Talent Show	20	21 Campers Leave
22 Camp is Closed	23	24	25	26	27	28
29	30	31				

1. How many days long is camp?

    a) 10 days   **b)** 14 days   **c)** 9 days

2. On what day is the trip to the lake?

    a) Wednesday **b)** Sunday **c)** Thursday

3. What comes first, the hayride or the talent show?

    a) talent show   **b)** hayride

4. Which activity on the calendar would you most like to do?

_____

_____

Clean-up Time!

Add the marbles. Write the number on the bag.

1. +  =

2.  + =

3.  + =

4.  +  =

5. +  =

Subtracting Stones

Count the number of stones in each box. Then take away
one stone and write the total on the line.

1.

$$4 \quad - \quad 1 \quad = \quad 3$$

2.

$$5 \quad - \quad 1 \quad = \underline{\quad}$$

3.

$$6 \quad - \quad 1 \quad = \underline{\quad}$$

You Can Read!

Read each word. Then draw a picture to
match on a separate piece of paper.

cat   ball   nest   ring

pig   mop   rope   drum

Money Match

Circle the coin on each ladder that matches the coin at the top.

Picture Puzzle

Draw a line to the matching half of each picture.
Your line will pass through the matching letters.

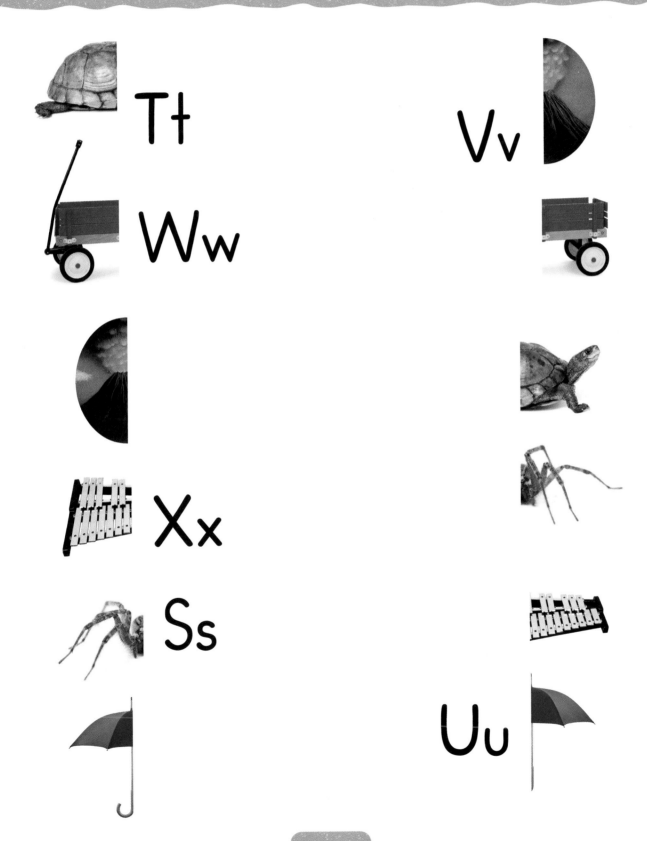

Ride the Coaster

Read the sentences. Draw a line to the picture that matches.

1. It is early morning.

2. Rita and her dad drive to a theme park.

3. The roller coaster is their first ride.

4. Rita is happy. She thinks the park is a lot of fun.

Big Balloons!

Read the word on each hot air balloon.

If the word is the name of an animal, circle the balloon with **GREEN**.

If the word is the name of a place, circle the balloon with **BLUE**.

If the word is the name of a person, circle the balloon with **PURPLE**.

School Day Subtraction

How many days did each child go to school?
A box with an X means the child was absent that day.

1.

MON	TUE	WED	THU	FRI
1	2	3	4̷	5̷

5 − 2 = 3

2.

MON	TUE	WED	THU	FRI
1̸	2	3̸	4̸	5

_____

3.

MON	TUE	WED	THU	FRI
1	2̸	3̸	4̸	5̸

_____

Vowel Match

Circle the matching vowel in each row.

a	e a o
e	i u e
i	i a u
o	u a o
u	e u o

Find Your Way!

Follow the instructions below.

Use **RED** to trace a path from the to the .

Use **BLUE** to trace a path from the to the .

Use **GREEN** to trace a path from the to the .

Use **YELLOW** to trace a path from the to the .

How Do They Feel?

Look at the pictures of the kids at a theme park. Can you guess how they are feeling? Use the words in the box to label each picture.

| scared | sad | happy | excited |

1.

excited

2.

3.

4.

All Around the Clock

Find the clocks, then draw a line from each to the middle.

$1.00

22
Main Street

The Lost Yo-yo

Follow the trail of **Yy** letter pairs to solve the maze and see who lost the yo-yo!

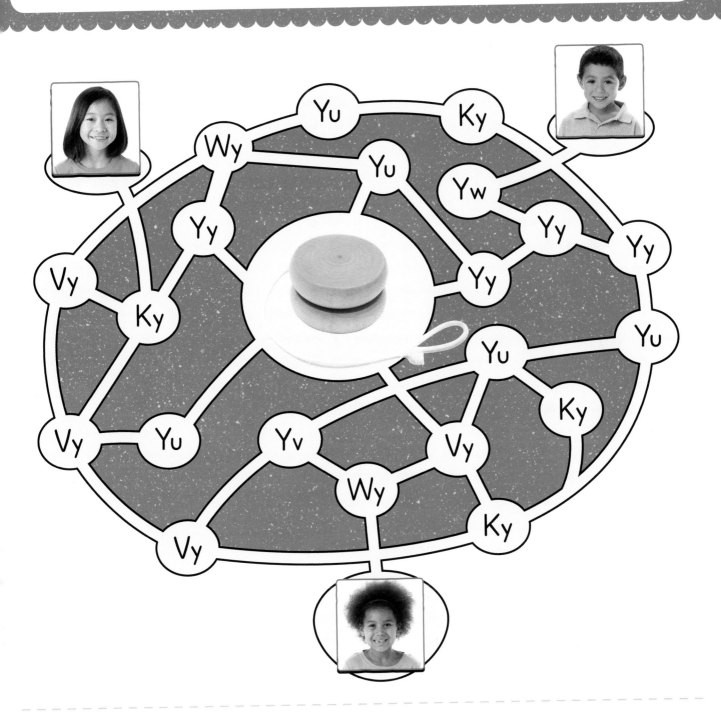

Trace and write.

As Big as the Sun

Write the names of the sunflower parts. Use words from the word box.

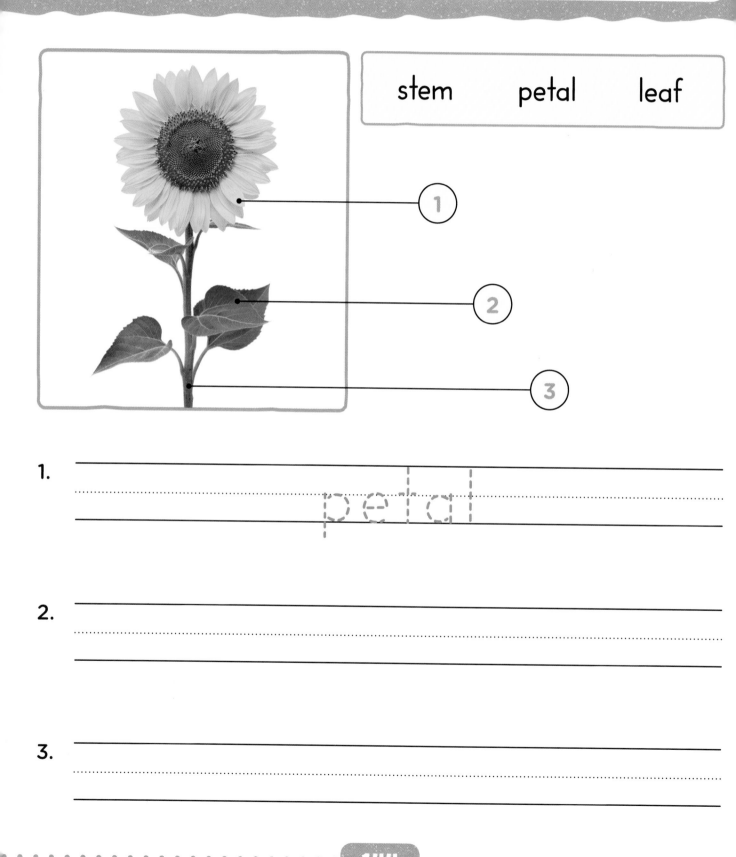

stem   petal   leaf

1. petal

2.

3.

Subtraction Signs

How many cars are left? Count the cars, then subtract and write the sum.

1.

2.

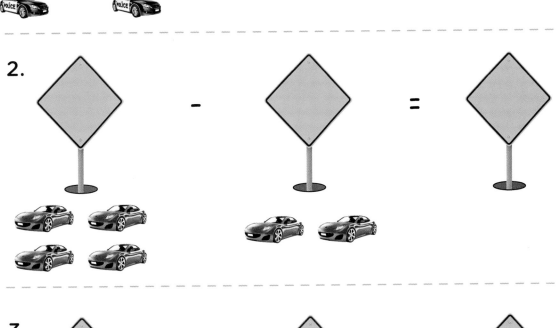

3.

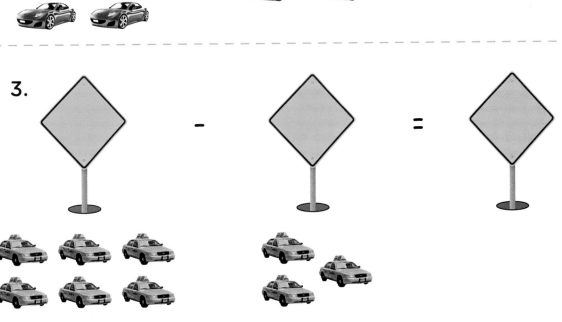

Z Is for Zebra

Find the row that has **Zz** three times and circle it.

Ss	Zx	Zz
Zz	Zz	Zs
Zz	Sz	Zz

Trace the letters **Zz**.

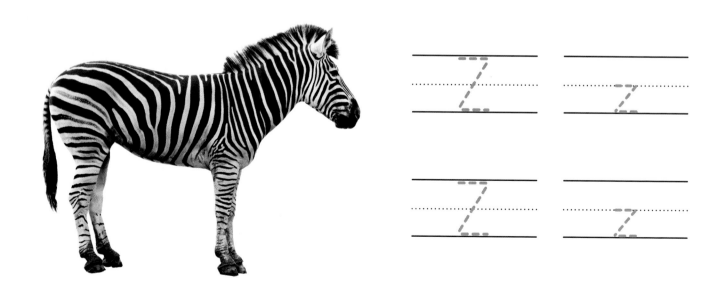

Pretty Patterns

Color the pictures to finish the patterns.

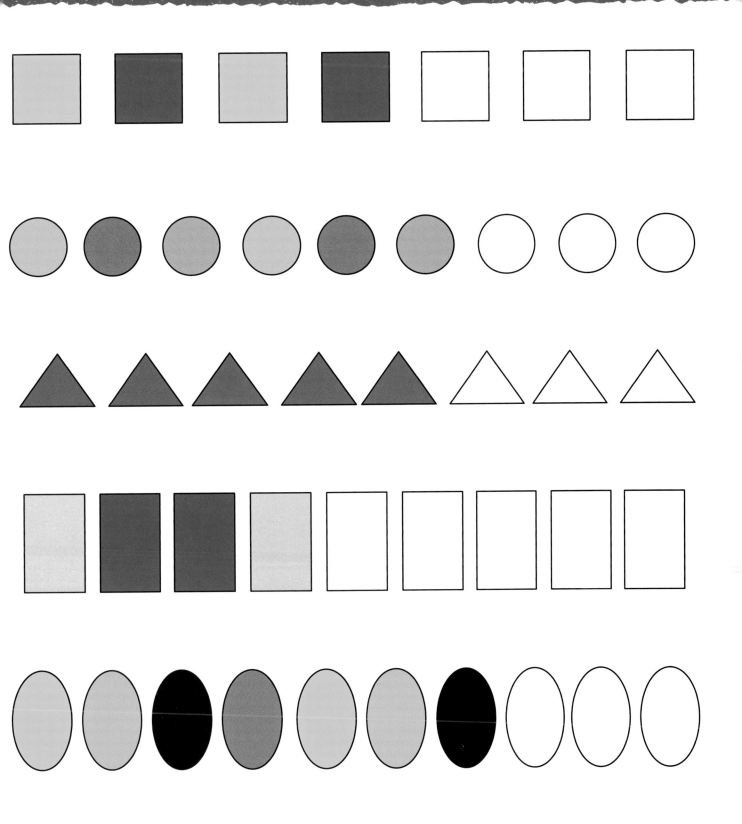

An Apple a Day

Read the story. Then draw a picture of Johnny Appleseed in the box below.

Johnny Appleseed was a kind man. He planted apple trees. He loved nature and animals. Johnny Appleseed made many friends.

Penny Lane

Count the number of pennies along each lane and write the total.

1.  _____ 7¢ _____

2.  _____ ¢ _____

3.  _____ ¢ _____

4.  _____ ¢ _____

Y and Z

Circle the objects that begin with the letter **Y** or the letter **Z**.

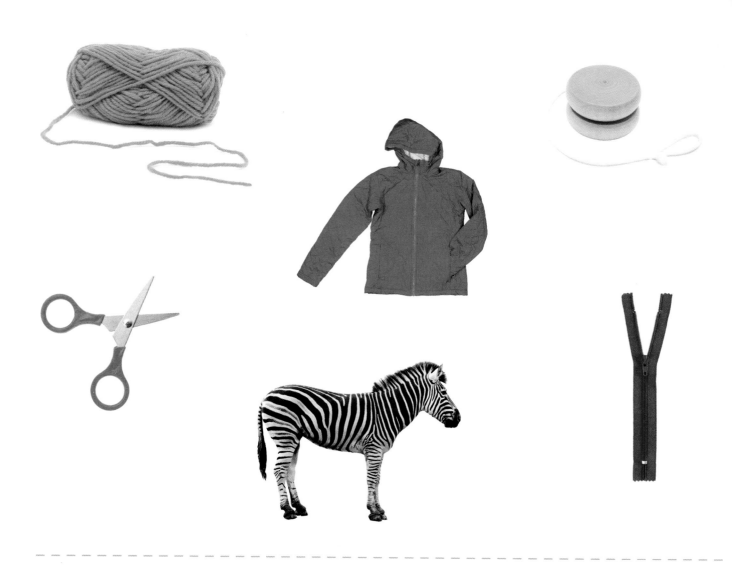

Trace and write.

Yy

Zz

Summer Story

Draw a picture of something you did this summer. Then have an adult help you write a sentence to go with your picture.

So Long, Summer!

Summer is almost over. Cross out the pictures of summer things.
Circle the pictures of fall things.

Size Wise

Circle the shape on each ladder that matches the size of the top shape.

Story Scene

Tell a story to go along with the picture. Help an adult
write your story on the lines below.

_____

....

_____

_____

....

_____

_____

....

_____

March Math

Count the pictures on the calendar. Then add or subtract below.

MARCH

SUN	MON	TUE	WED	THU	FRI	SAT
			1	2	3	4
5	6	7	8	9	10	11
12	13	14	15	16	17	18
19	20	21	22	23	24	25
26	27	28	29	30	31	

1. ☀ _5_ + ☁ _2_ = _7_

2. 🌧 ___ + ☁ ___ = ___

3. ☀ ___ - ☁ ___ = ___

4. 🌧 ___ - ☁ ___ = ___

Answer Key

Page 4

Page 5

Page 6

Page 7
2. 8
3. 3
4. 7
5. 4

Page 8

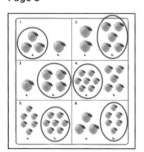

Page 9

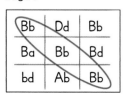

Page 10
The star comes next.

Page 11

Page 12
The page is completed when all the letters are traced.

Page 13

Page 14
These objects should be circled:
feather
beach ball
straw
leaf

Page 15

Page 16

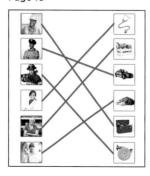

Page 17
The calendar is complete when all of the numbers have been traced.
1. 2
2. 1
3. 3

Page 18

Page 19
2. 12
3. 5
4. 20
5. 14

Page 20

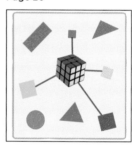

Page 21

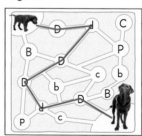

Page 22

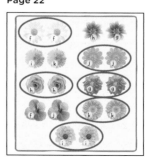

Page 23
1. m
2. p
3. t
4. u
5. z

Page 24

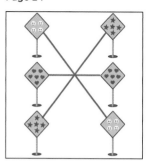

Page 25

Ee	Ce	Fe
Ff	Ec	Ee
Ee	Ee	Ee

Page 26
These objects should be circled:
daisy
parakeet
dog

Page 27

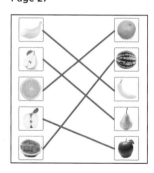

Page 28

Page 29
These objects should be circled:
fish
feather
flower
fan

Page 30
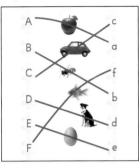

Page 31
These objects should be circled:
baseball
button
soccer ball
sun

Page 32
Numbers 8, 12, 14, 16, 20, and 26 should be filled in on the calendar. Placement of cakes will vary.

Page 33
This page is complete when all the lines and letters are traced and a new line is drawn.

Page 34

Page 35
The uncolored object in each row should be colored:
1. green
2. yellow
3. blue
4. yellow
5. purple

Page 36

Page 37

Page 38
This page is complete when all the letters are traced.

Page 39
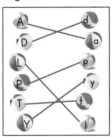

Page 40
1. 8
2. 9
3. 7

Page 41

Hh	Hh	Ih
Ed	Hh	Hh
Hh	Hh	Hb

Page 42
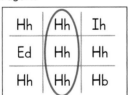

Page 43

Page 44
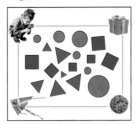

Page 45
These objects should be circled:
igloo
ice cream
ice cube

Page 46

Page 47
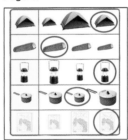

Page 48
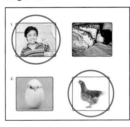

Page 49
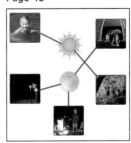

Page 50
2. d
3. b
4. f
5. b
6. t

Page 51
The calendar is complete when the numbers have been traced and 2 and 5 have been filled in. There are 7 days of vacation.

Page 52

Page 53
2. Dd
3. Ww
4. Pp
5. Gg
6. Bb
7. Kk

Page 54

Page 55
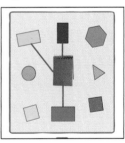

Page 56
These objects should be circled:
jet
jar
jug
jacket

Page 57
This page is completed when drawing is complete.

Page 58
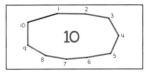

Page 59

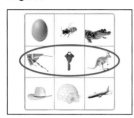

Page 60

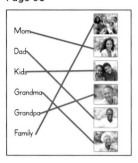

Page 61

Page 62
These objects should be circled:
ladybug
lantern
leaf
lemonade

Page 63
These objects should be circled:
pyramid
tepee
party hat

Page 64
2. a
3. d
4. b

Page 65

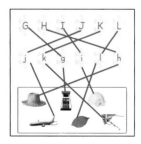

Page 66

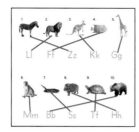

Page 67

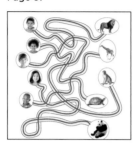

Page 68
Numbers 1, 3, 6, and 8 should be filled in.
Baseball glove = 4
Soccer ball = 8

Page 69

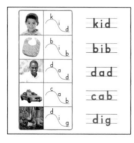

Page 70

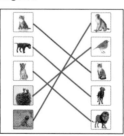

Page 71
1. a
2. a
3. b

Page 72
1. a
2. a
3. b
4. a

Page 73

Page 74

Page 75
2. 15

Page 76

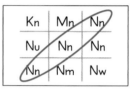

Page 77

Page 78

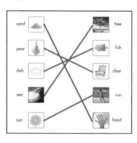

Page 79

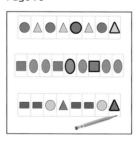

Page 80
These objects should be circled:
orange
owl
octopus
ostrich

Page 81
1. D
2. F, H
3. K, M

Page 82
1. p
2. s, t
3. v, y

Page 83
Answers will vary.

Page 84
These objects should be circled:
kite
jet
bird
balloon
bee

Page 85
These objects should have clouds drawn around them:
pelican
seagull
These objects should have waves drawn under them:
dolphin
starfish
fish
walrus
whale

Page 86

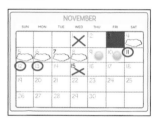

Page 87

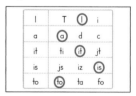

Page 88
1. a
2. a
3. a

Page 89
2. 17
3. 23
4. 30
5. 14
6. 11
8. 23
9. 15
10. 19
11. 25
12. 9
14. 6
15. 17
16. 27
17. 15
18. 10

Page 90
1. b
2. b
3. a
4. a

Page 91

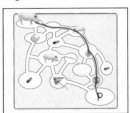

Page 92
2. 6
3. 4
4. 3
5. 8
6. 5

Page 93
2. 8
3. 7
4. 5
5. 9
6. 4

Page 94
Page is completed when numbers are traced and written.

Page 95

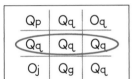

Page 96

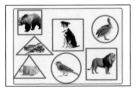

Page 97

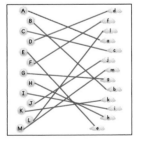

Page 98
These objects should be circled:
rain
rock
roller skate
rainbow

Page 99

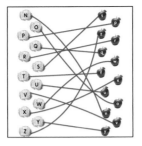

Page 100

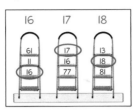

Page 101

Page 102
1. c, f, g
2. j, l, o
3. q, t, v, w
4. y

Page 103
2. 3, 4 (circle 4)
3. 5, 3 (circle 5)
4. 2, 5 (circle 5)

Page 104

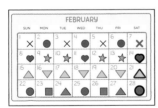

Page 105
4–5. Answers will vary.

Page 106

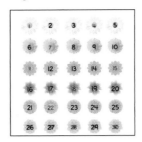

Page 107

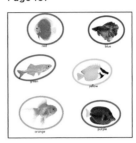

Page 108
1. a
2. a
3. b
4. b

Page 109
Pictures will vary.

Page 110
The page is completed when the words are traced and written on the lines.

Page 111

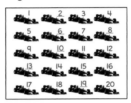

Page 112

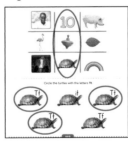

Page 113

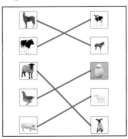

Page 114
2. c
3. a
4. b
5. a

Page 115
2. 5
3. 6

Page 116
These objects should be circled:
umbrella
unicorn
unicycle

Page 117
2. respect
3. Earth
4. manners

Page 118
2. b
3. b
4. c
5. b
6. a

Page 119
2, 4
3, 1
Bottom of page: Answers will vary.

Page 120
The page is completed when the words are traced and written on the lines.

Page 121
1. a
2. b
3. a
4. Pictures will vary.

Page 122
3 + 1 = 4

Page 123

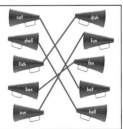

Page 124

Page 125
1. b
2. a

Page 126

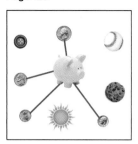

Page 127
2. fall
3. summer
4. spring

Page 128
2. 2 + 4 = 6
3. 3 + 3 = 6

Page 129

Ww	Vw	Wv
Ww	WW	Xw
Ww	Ww	Wy

Page 130
1. b
2. a
3. b
4. Answers will vary.

Page 131
2. 4
3. 13
4. 12
5. 10

Page 132
2. 4
3. 5

Page 133
Pictures will vary.

Page 134

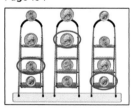

Page 135

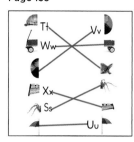

Page 136

Page 137

Page 138
2. 5 – 3 = 2
3. 5 – 4 = 1

Page 139

a	e	ⓐ	o
e	i	u	ⓔ
i	ⓘ	a	u
o	u	a	ⓞ
u	e	ⓤ	o

Page 140
Paths can vary but may include:

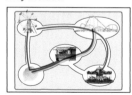

Page 141
2. sad
3. scared
4. happy

Page 142

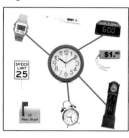

Page 143

Page 144
2. leaf
3. stem

Page 145
2. 4 – 2 = 2
3. 6 – 3 = 3

Page 146

Ss	Zx	Zz
Zz	Zz	Zs
Zz	Sz	Zz

Page 147

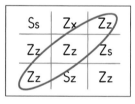

Page 148
Pictures will vary.

Page 149
2. 4
3. 8
4. 5

Page 150
These objects should be circled:
yarn
yo-yo
zebra
zipper

Page 151
Pictures and sentences will vary.

Page 152

Page 153

Page 154
Stories will vary.

Page 155
2. 4 + 2 = 6
3. 5 – 2 = 3
4. 4 – 2 = 2

Image Credits

All images by Depositphotos, Dreamstime, iStockphoto, Shutterstock, Thinkstock, and Wikimedia Foundation, with the following exception: © Dorling Kindersley/Getty Images (map).